ONE BEAD AT A TIME

a memoir

Beverly Little Thunder

as told to Sharron Proulx-Turner

INANNA
Memoir Series

Published in Canada by
Inanna Publications and Education Inc.
210 Founders College, York University
4700 Keele Street, Toronto, Ontario M3J 1P3
Telephone: (416) 736-5356 Fax (416) 736-5765
Email: inanna.publications@inanna.ca Website: www.inanna.ca

 Canada Council Conseil des Arts
for the Arts du Canada  ONTARIO ARTS COUNCIL

We gratefully acknowledge the support of the Canada Council for the Arts and the Ontario Arts Council for our publishing program. We also acknowledge the financial support of the Government of Canada through the Canada Book Fund.

Printed and Bound in Canada.

Cover photograph of Beverly Little Thunder: Jane English
Cover design: Val Fullard

Library and Archives Canada Cataloguing in Publication

Little Thunder, Beverly, author
        One bead at a time : a memoir / by Beverly Little Thunder, as told to Sharron Proulx-Turner.

(Inanna memoir series)
Issued in print and electronic formats.
ISBN 978-1-77133-265-1 (paperback).-- ISBN 978-1-77133-266-8 (epub). -- ISBN 978-1-77133-268-2 (pdf)

        1. Little Thunder, Beverly. 2. Lakota Indians—Biography. 3. Two-spirit people—North America—Biography. 4. Indian women activists—North America—Biography. 5. Indian leadership—North America. I. Proulx-Turner, Sharron, editor II. Title. III. Series: Inanna memoir series

E99.T34L58 2016   978.004'9752440092   C2016-900715-4
                                                        C2016-900716-2

 MIX
Paper from
responsible sources
FSC
www.fsc.org   FSC® C004071

*For all the women
who have learned to believe in themselves.*

TABLE OF CONTENTS

FOREWORD

Where Dreams are for People
What Water is for Trees

THIS IS HOW I SEE Beverly Little Thunder's and Pam Alexander's land in traditional Abenaki territory, held in trust for time immemorial for women's ceremony. A place where prayers are answered and dreams are born on the wetlands of the Green Mountains in Vermont. Kunsi Keya Tamakoci. Grandmother Turtle, a place where the Creator's presence resonates and women's and children's lives are transformed. Their voices lifted in song, their laughter, their tears and secrets remain with that land, year after year. Not just because the trips "back to the land" from the cities remind people to slow down. Witnessing seventy to one hundred women work together to prepare annually for ceremony, sitting with those one hundred women to eat, circling with them to introduce themselves one by one, that is the power of this place. Everyone is there to pray. Many are there to seek healing.

My name is Sharron Proulx-Turner. I am a member of the Métis Nation of Alberta. Among many other things, I am a Métisse Nokomis (grandmother), community worker, storyteller, poet, writer. I spent eleven of my summers and most of those winters on the steep Kunsi Keya wetlands. There were rain storms and storm warnings and wind damage. Collapsed water-soaked kitchens. Line ups of sopping wet women and children, laughing together in the pouring down rain, their voices resonating through the mature forest that holds the land, their rhythms settling in the wet air like the lightning bugs that grace the grasses and the ground-covered fern. I will always remember the young Indigenous mommies and their babies. They found a home.

And home is what Kunsi Keya is to Beverly Little Thunder, a Lakota woman from Standing Rock, who followed a vision that brought her from the deserts in California to this eastern woodland. Her vision is more than thirty years old now and has realized itself to some extent. Any meeting place for women is at risk of being called "New Age" by the media, especially a place where an Indigenous woman dares to follow what she was shown by Creator and her Elders. Dares open up ceremony to women, to transgender, lesbian, bisexual, queer—all who identify as women. Dares include non-Indigenous women in the foundation building of the land, welcome them as helpers at almost all levels. But there is nothing New Age about what happens on this land. What happens on this land is sacred Lakota women's ceremony. Sacrifice. Growth. Peacefulness. Fun. Healing.

Beverly wanted to tell her story. She heard I am a writer and asked me if I would write her story. I told her, no. Your story is not mine to write, it is yours. But I am not a writer, Beverly would say. Me? As my Aunty would say, if you can talk, you can sing. And if you can sing, you can write. We decided that Beverly would relay her story to me by audio-tape and I would be both witness in the moment and transcribe her words later. Play. Stop. Listen. Write. Play. Stop. Play. Stop. Listen. Write. Word. For. Word. Laboriously and literally years later, we had almost 900 pages of text, too long for a book. So I began the job of editing. Of staying true to Beverly's oral word and being inclusive enough with each of her stories (sometimes told several times throughout the tapes).

I was fortunate. I received a Canada Council International Aboriginal grant to begin the project (2009) with Beverly on Kunsi Keya land in Vermont, and later two Canada Council/Alberta Initiative grants to help complete the transcribing and editing here at home in Alberta. That took years. Then to find a publisher. Inanna Publications was recommended to me at a conference where I was a guest reader. The story continues from there. Luciana Ricciutelli with Inanna has been incredible, not only in her careful and precise edits, but in the loving care taken with this book, with the author. Such an exciting moment for Beverly Little Thunder, another part of her vision fulfilled.

Recently, I was diagnosed with end-stage liver cancer. I was having some pain, had an ultrasound thinking I had a gallbladder problem (given I'm the only adult in my large family who has a gallbladder), but no. Not so. This book may close my life. Life is story. I became involved in this project, not because I love impossible work, but to give back to the Indigenous women and children whose stories so often go untold. To give back to the spirits of the Indigenous women and children who have been and still are missing or murdered. For my mother and grandmothers before me, whose unspeakable sacrifices paved the way for me to be a writer. Thank you, grandmothers. Thank you, Creator.

—Sharron Proulx-Turner, MA
Calgary, Alberta, May, 2016

Beverly Little Thunder, 2000

1.

MY BEGINNINGS

IHANNI WASTE' THEY CALL ME. "She who can be depended upon." When I received this name, I was told not to repeat it in my language. It is my spirit name. The world knows me as Beverly Little Thunder, but those closest to me call me Unci, Lakota for grandmother. I am a Womon from the Standing Rock Band of the Lakota Nation. I am Oglala and Teton. This is my story.

MY GRANDMOTHER AND GREAT GRANDMOTHER

My grandmother and great-grandmother were from the Standing Rock reservation in North Dakota. They were both full bloods. My grandfather was from the Cheyenne River Agency, which was further south. He came from a family of ten boys and my grandmother talked about how she didn't even know my grandfather before she married him—he was quite a bit older than her. Her father and her mother told her that she was going to get married on a Sunday after church. Her grandmother started putting together a dress for her made out of flour sacs.

One Saturday they went to town and there were a whole bunch of men standing over by where the horses were tied. Her mother, my great-grandmother, said, "You're going to marry one of the Marshall boys." My grandmother said she and her sister looked over the men, trying to figure out which one she was going to marry, and of course, which one was more handsome, and which one neither wanted to marry. She said she really had no idea who her husband would be until they got to the church. After the mass, her mother told her to stay seated, then the priest came, the Marshalls walked in, and she met my grandfather. She talked about how in those days that's the way they did it; your parents who decided for you. You didn't have long courtships. She said, sometimes, if you were lucky, you found someone that you liked and your parents would agree, and then you were able to marry him.

THE BIRTH OF MY MOTHER

My grandmother had her first child, Christina—my mother— on Christmas. There was a snow storm that day, so my mom was born at home. My grandmother said that my mother was very, very sick and they had to call a medicine man to come. He stayed at the house for several days to doctor her. She recovered, and it was really important that she get well because she was the first girl born in the Marshall family. Every one of those ten Marshall boys, she said, had nothing but boys. Each one of those boys had about eight sons and nobody had a daughter. My mother was the first. But my mother became like my grandfather's first-born son because she was his first-born child, and she talked about how she spent most of her time with her father, not my grandmother.

When my mother was four, she was sent away to a government school and she and my Aunt Gloria, my mothers' best friend, used to talk about how when they got to the school, they were the two youngest there, and all the older girls looked out for them. But one day they were playing and she and Gloria were talking in Lakota. They were reprimanded and forced to stay in broom closets overnight. In later years, when my Aunt Gloria was about sixty, I remember sitting in the kitchen with my aunt and my mom when my aunt started talking about that time. She began crying and said, "Christina, what could we as four-year-old little girls have been talking about that was so horrible that they would treat us in such a poor manner and put babies in closets, because we were just babies, Christina." My mom began to cry too. It's the only time I saw my mother cry. I became aware of the damage that government schools did to our people as I witnessed that episode. I sat there and didn't say a word. I just listened.

My mother did talk about being in boarding school and how she never knew her mother. Because her family could not afford for her to travel back and forth, she was always a part of the group of kids who stayed at the school even during holidays, so she never spent a Christmas or a birthday or anything at home from the time she was four. She only came home in the summer, when she would help my grandfather with the cattle and the farm. She said she was much closer to my grandfather than she was to my grandmother. I have pictures of my mother and grandmother sitting together, and the look on my mother's face is one of a wistful child looking at her mother, trying to get her attention and my grandmother instead is staring straight into the camera, as if my mother was not there. I think the government schools really damaged their relationship, and as a result, my mother was not a very good mother to me.

THE BIRTH OF MY FATHER

My father was raised in an orphanage run by two German women. When the orphanage closed, they adopted him because no one else had. He was given the last name of Skillens. There was no information on his mother. They knew nothing about her, and the document that I saw said that he was born on the steps of a hospital in Illinois or Indiana, that his mother had died in childbirth, and that he was a male. It didn't indicate how much he weighed, or how long he was, and even the time of birth was not recorded. His mother was described as being about five-foot-five, weighing about one hundred and twenty-five pounds, with long dark hair, brown eyes, and an olive complexion, possibly twenty-three, twenty-four. That's all the information he had. So he didn't know much about his mother, and he knew even less about who his father was.

My father met my mother when my mother was in the army. He was in the Merchant Marines because, not having a birth certificate, he couldn't get into the military service. At that time, my mother was going to school at Haskell, and then she got a scholarship to go to Kansas City University. After her second year, she had to declare a major. She wanted to go into interior design but she was told that, as an Indian, she couldn't be an art major, that the scholarship was only valid if she was going to be a nurse or a teacher. She bluntly stated, "I don't like children and I don't like blood," then quit university and joined the Women's Army Corps. She talked about the racism she experienced during that time. She was put in a barracks with Black women because there were two barracks: one for the white women, and one for the Black women. When she arrived to check in, her superior officer called her into his office, together with her cousin Sophie, who had joined with her. He pulled out a headdress and asked them to pose with him while he took pictures. He talked about how he was sure he had a little Native blood in him somewhere and said he was so proud to have two Native girls in his division. I was horrified as she told this story. I was livid for her. To her, it was just what had happened.

As I grew up, my mother told me I should never marry a Native man, that I should always try to find a white man because that would give me some status in the world. For a good part of my growing up, that was her mantra: Be as good as the white person. That changed, but not until later on.

MY EARLY YEARS

I weighed three pounds and two ounces when I was born. I had to spend three months in the hospital before I could come home. During those three months, I didn't have a name and it's reflected on my birth certificate that my name wasn't registered until three months later, in March. I don't know if my mother came to visit during that time. She never said.

My mother was very cold emotionally. She was not affectionate. I only heard her say "I love you" to me once in my entire life. She was very good at using the belt. She was physically abusive. I never understood whether it was me that she didn't like, or if she was just mean. I didn't want to believe that she was just mean, so I internalized that it was me. She would often say to me, "You're ugly, you're stupid, you're never going to find a husband."

On the other hand, my father adored me. He said that I was the most beautiful girl, that I was smart, and that some day he would buy me fifty-dollar dresses. Why fifty-dollar dresses, I don't know, but that was his goal. My father was a labourer. He was not a professional person. He'd only gone as far as the third grade. He taught himself to read and write and in the process, taught me to read and write. So at the age of three, I was able to read all of the kindergarten and first-grade books that were later given to me to read in school. By then, I was bored because I'd already read them.

We were very poor, but I didn't see myself as poor. I thought that everybody lived the way we lived. We never had a matching set of dishes; we had broken, chipped, mismatched plates. My mother used to buy oatmeal in a box where you got a free dish, so we had various dishes from different boxes of oatmeal. We also had jelly jars and pickle jars—my mother liked pickles, so we had lots of pickle jars—which we drank out of.

My father was a very good baker, and every Saturday he would clear the kitchen table, flour it up, and make bread for the whole week. He would always say, "Oh, I have extra dough and I don't know what to do with it. Maybe I'll make cinnamon rolls." If we were lucky, we'd have raisins. I think now that he always knew how much dough he was making, but he always made it seem like he had extra and that it was a special treat. He would put the cinnamon rolls in a big crock and all week long that was our dessert. Fruit cocktail and graham crackers, too. Those were the sweets we had when I was growing up.

We lived in rooming houses, but when I was born we lived in a garage. I was due in February but I was born early. My mother had wanted to go to a New Year's party. They called a taxi— in those days most people didn't have cars. They were in Los Angeles. They got into a taxi and she started having labour pains so she asked to go to a hospital instead. They were taken to the closest hospital, but then were redirected to the county hospital. When she got there, they gave her some medication to try to stop the labour, but the labour continued and I was born at 11:47 p.m., New Year's Eve. She always said that I was so impatient.

If I had waited thirteen more minutes, I could have been the first baby born in 1948. I didn't weigh much when I was born, but I've made up for it. It must have been a crazy night is all I can say because years later—all her life—my mother told the story of me being born on New Year's Eve.

When my parents took me home, my grandmother wanted them to return to Standing Rock and bring me with them, but my mom didn't want to travel because I was so small. My parents went back to the garage that they were living in then. But my father and mother had these friends, Bea and Calvin, who were living in a one-room apartment in a house. They moved themselves and all their stuff into the garage and then moved my parents and me into their apartment in the house so that my parents wouldn't have live in a garage with a baby. Aunt Bea and Uncle Calvin became like my relatives when I was very little.

Both my mom and father were in government boarding schools back in the thirties. There were always diseases to contend with in the schools. In the fifties, it was polio. Every kid had to get polio shots. But back in the thirties, it was rickets—caused by a lack of vitamin D—so somebody decided that fish oil, or fish, was a good source of vitamin D. Cod liver oil came on the market. It was probably on the market before then, but it was introduced to the government schools at that time, probably the cheapest supplement the schools could use, so all the kids used to get a tablespoon of cod liver oil every morning before breakfast.

When I was born my father decided that since I was so small, if one tablespoon made you healthy, then two would be better. So every morning when I woke up he gave me two tablespoons of cod liver oil and to this day, at sixty-three years old, I do not eat fish. I have had fish prepared for me in many wonderful ways. I'll take a bite, and it doesn't taste bad, but I can't get beyond that. I will probably die never eating fish. Recently, I started taking an omega-3 capsule, because my daughter insisted. But it's only because it doesn't taste like fish, and I don't burp fish. The first time I burp fish, I told my daughter, that will be the end of it. My father wanted me to be healthy. He made sure that having been born at three-and-a-half pounds, I was going to thrive. Now, at two hundred and ten pounds, I want him to know, I have thrived.

My dad is the one I remember the most growing up. He was very affectionate and a lot of fun to be around. He was also a very compassionate person. When he got a paycheck, he would always buy chewing gum and chocolate bars. He kept them in a box in his drawer. About once a month, he would take the bus and he would go to a local orphanage. He would take the chocolate bars and the chewing gum to the kids there and he would spend the afternoon with them. He took me with him several times. He said it was because when he was in the orphanage, no one ever came to see him, and he wanted to go and see the kids. I always wondered if my mother was even aware that my dad visited the orphanage. She never acknowledged it, or never said, "Your dad's doing this." She'd just get mad at him when he was getting dressed.

My dad was a spiffy dresser. He only wore wool pants, and they had to be navy blue. He also wore a double-breasted suit jacket and a white shirt. He didn't like ties, so he didn't wear a tie. He would wear steel-toe work boots because he worked in a warehouse, in a factory. But that's the way he went to work. He said, you can't get on the bus looking all dumpy; you have to get on the bus looking nice. It wasn't until he was in his fifties that we managed to get him into sweat pants, but even so, he wouldn't leave the house in them. He had to change his clothes. You knew when he pulled out a clean shirt, that he was getting ready to go somewhere. And my dad never drove. He took the bus.

My father always said that what you put out comes back to you. It's always been that way. I remember one time when I was in high school, my father went down to the small local store where they had credit, and he got a turkey and all the trimmings for Thanksgiving dinner. He took it to this woman who lived down the street from us. My mother got very angry. She thought he was having an affair with this woman. He said, no, that she got laid off work, that she had four kids, and that it was Thanksgiving. "She needs it," he said. Oh, my mom was not happy. Even I wondered how my father met this woman. Well, it turns out he met her waiting at the bus. She used to wait for the bus with him all the time and they would ride the bus together. She got off a couple of stops before he did so they struck up a friendship. Her husband had died and she had all these kids. My dad wanted to do something to help her. He put up with my mother, all of her accusations, and rantings and ravings. He just said, "Chris, there've been times when we needed help and we've gotten help." I always remember that. To this day, I will always help a family out on the holidays. I go out of my way to provide food and gifts for children that don't have them, usually a single mom. I know how hard it can be to provide those things for your children when you're a single mom.

When he was about fifty-five, my dad discovered he had a tumour behind his eye. It was cancerous and they had to remove his eye. He was given a glass eye to replace it. Five years later he died of cancer. Had he been going to the doctor on a regular basis, they probably would have caught the cancer soon and given him aggressive treatment, but he didn't believe in going to doctors unless it was an absolute emergency. By the time he got there, he was too far gone for them to do anything. They told us that he was full of cancer and that it had spread into all his organs. They said he had about three months to live. He lived three days, and then he was gone. My dad was a pretty incredible person. He was one of the loves of my life.

THE FIRE

By the time I was five, my mother had had my sister, Laurel. She's three years younger than I am. Eleven months later she had my brother Randy, and I don't even think it was even ten months later that she had my brother Ronny. Right after Ronny was born—he was about three months old—we moved into a rooming house. There was a roll-away bed that my sister, brother and I slept on, and in the corner, there was a little basket for my baby brother Ronny. My father and mother slept on the couch, which turned into sort of a bed you could flatten out. It didn't have a bed inside it like couches do now; it just folded forward and you lay it down on the ground and made it a bed. My father was lying on that couch one night and my mother was out somewhere. It was about three in the morning when I woke up. There was a cloud above my head—it was smoke. The air was very dry. I had to go to the bathroom. We shared a bathroom with a neighbour and to get to the bathroom, I had to go outside to the back porch and then down a few steps. Instead, I went over to my father on the couch-bed to wake him. He no sooner sat up that the whole couch went up in flames.

My dad opened the door and started yelling for help and then he ran into the kitchen and tried to get something to put water on the fire. It all happened so fast. I watched the flames, watched them leap from the couch to the chairs to the curtains. It was pretty scary. I was five years old. The only way I knew how to get out was through the front door. It was latched at the top and the only way I could reach the latch was to stand on the arm of the couch, which was now in flames.

So, when my dad jumped up off the couch, I got scared, and ran back to the rollaway bed. I had a little blanket and I was trying to get my little brother out of the basket. My father was outside yelling. People started coming in and somebody grabbed my sister and then somebody came back in and grabbed my brother from upstairs. They were yelling at my father to shut the door so the fire wouldn't spread, and they slammed the door. A man, a sailor walking by—coming home from the bar because bars in Los Angeles closed at two a.m. then—ran to the side of the building where there were vines growing up. He climbed those vines and the trellises to get to our second story window. He broke the window with his arm, broke his arm in the process, and got my brother and I out. He held us outside, out from his body with his good arm and held the vine with his broken arm until the fire truck got there and was able to take us down. I have a scar under my arm that looks like a big brown birth mark. I was burning and the man had to slap me with his hands until the fire went out under my arm.

I still don't know where my mother was the night of the fire. I guess she came home the next morning when the fire was put out. My baby brother, Ronnie, got sick. He'd gotten a lot of smoke in his lungs. He got pneumonia. I remember him crying and crying and crying, and my mother walking him, my father walking him, and still they couldn't get him to stop crying. Then, in the middle of the night, my mother woke me up and said, "We're taking

Ronnie to the hospital. We'll lock the door after we go and you can sleep on the couch." I was feeling very grown up.

It was light outside when they got home. My mother came in the house and walked by me. I said, "Momma? Where's Ronnie?" She turned around and said, "Ronnie's dead and it's your entire fault." Then she ran out of the room. My father came in after her. I was excited because I didn't know what dead meant. I asked my dad, "Where's Ronnie?" He said, "Well, Ronnie died and he went to be with the angels. He was too sick and the doctors couldn't fix him." I still didn't know what that meant. There was no funeral. There was no closure.

My mother became very bitter. She had gone to the local Catholic Church to try and get some assistance to bury him, but because he had not been baptized, they wouldn't bury him and they wouldn't help her because she hadn't been coming to mass at that church. That's when I remember starting to see my mother drink a lot. I remember seeing bottles of beer sitting on the table all the time. I carried that with me for many years—that I was responsible for my brother's death. Although, as an adult, I knew intellectually I wasn't responsible for that, emotionally, the child in me could still hear my mother saying that to me. It only confirmed the feelings I had that my mom didn't like me. Of course she didn't like me—I killed my brother. It made perfect sense to me.

AFTER THE FIRE

More terrifying than being in that burning building was when a few days later we had to sleep in that room again. We had nowhere else to go. Someone had brought some mattresses and placed them on the floor. Everything else around us was charred. I remember being so afraid to go to sleep. I was afraid I was going to wake up and we would be in flames again.

Soon afterward, as an emergency measure, we were moved into a housing project. The Red Cross helped and got us some furniture and household stuff. That was a "move up" for us, I guess. It was the first time that we actually had two bedrooms, a living room, and a kitchen. It was small, but it was our home. A few weeks after we had moved in, I was playing in the house on a Sunday morning when my father asked me to go and see if the paperboy was coming. I went outside and had to walk down a walkway and then down some stairs to the roadway, where I saw a little boy on a bicycle who had canvas bags over his bicycle. In the sunlight, is hair looked fuzzy and all burnt up. I didn't know what his burnt back looked like, but that's what I imagined.

I went screaming into the house and told my father there was a little boy outside who'd been in a fire and that he was all burned up. My father ran out the door and came back in, and said, "It's okay. It's all right. He's not hurt." Then, without explaining, or saying anything, he grabbed two mayonnaise jars and said, "Go pick some flowers for your mother. I'm going make her some breakfast."

I went back outside and the first thing I saw were yellow mustard flowers, so I pulled out a bunch and brought them to my dad. He put them all in one jar, got some water, and then said, "Are there any others out there? Maybe different colours?" So I went out again and stole a rose from the neighbour, some oleander, more mustard flowers and whatever other flowers I could find along the road that weren't yellow. I brought them back and he put them in the other jar. After he'd filled the jar with water, then he said, "Well, which one do you think is the prettiest?"

I pondered for a minute and I was partial to the rose, so I said, "Oh, I kind of like the rose." I was probably really proud that I got away with stealing that one, so I said, "The one with all the different colour flowers."

My father said, "You know, when the Creator made the world, he thought that the world would look more beautiful with different colour flowers and he made people the same way. There are people all over the world who have different colour skin than we have. That little paperboy that you saw, his skin was very dark and he was probably from Africa. You're going to hear people call him the 'N' word." He went down this long list of terms that were derogatory for someone Black, and Black was one of those words, ironically.

He added, "I never ever want to hear you call anyone by those names. Those are bad names; those are bad words. Always use respect, and treat them with a lot of love and kindness because that's how they'll treat you."

I said, "Oh, okay." So that was my lesson about racism from my father. And you know, darn it, in the '70s when I started going to UCLA, it was during the time of Black Power and everybody wanted to be called Black. I had the hardest time calling them Black. I could still hear my father saying, "Never call anybody that." That was one of the memorable things that happened when we lived in that house.

GRANDMOTHER'S HOUSE

Every year I was taken to my grandmother's house, usually in early May, and then I would return home in the early fall. My mother would leave me there and I'd spend the summer with my grandmother. My grandmother was very much like my mom. She was very quiet. She didn't speak English when I was little. Everything she said was in Lakota, so I became fluent in Lakota. Unfortunately, as I grew older, I lost the language because there was no one else to talk to. But when I was a child, my cousins were always around. There was always a bunch of us, and we would sleep in this one big bed that was full of hay. It was basically a ticking full of hay. When it got flat my grandmother would just stuff more hay in it. I always thought hay was something really special until I found out it was just grass.

The summers at my grandmother's house are some of the happiest memories of my life. It was a good way for a kid to grow up, I think.

I remember going to church and bible school. One time I came home from Sunday school, got off the bus, and walked the quarter mile to the house, in tears. I climbed up the steps and my grandmother asked what was wrong. I told her that the minister said I was going to burn in hell.

She said, "Well, why?"

I replied, "Because he says if I'm not good, if I don't do what my mother tells me, then I'm going to die and burn in hell." I didn't know what it was to die yet because my brother hadn't passed, so I must have been about three-and-a-half, almost four.

I didn't know what hell was either. I just knew it was a place you went to burn.

My grandmother said, "No, that's not true. No, no, no—heaven and hell, that's for white people. Only white people go to heaven and hell."

So I thought about it for a minute and asked, "Oh, well, where do we go then?"

"If you're not good," she said, "and you don't do what your mother tells you, when a Lakota person dies, they come back in the next life as Navaho." I didn't know what a Navaho was then, but it must have been bad. I really tried to be good because I didn't want to be a Navaho.

Years and years later—my grandmother was about ninety-four—she didn't recognize us anymore. I was cutting vegetables and had all my silver bracelets on, and my turquoise, like the Navaho women wear. She turned to me and said, "Lila, Shicha." It means, "You're so bad."

I said, "What did I do, Grandma?"

She said, "You can't even wait until you've died. You're always practicing to be a Navaho."

I laughed because I realized that she remembered that from long ago. Who knows? Maybe I do have to come back as a Navaho. I haven't been that good.

THE CHICKS

My grandmother told some stories that I don't really remember well, but through her telling I can imagine the details. One of them was about how she used to get baby chicks in the mail. They would come in big flat crates. I remember one time being in the back of the wagon, and going into town with my cousins. We thought that was a great place to wrestle and play while my grandmother was driving the team. There'd be big boxes of baby chicks in the back with us. I remember poking my fingers in them, trying to get their attention.

My grandmother talked about how she went out into her barnyard afterwards and found a bunch of dead chicks. She thought, well, maybe they weren't healthy. Then the next day she went out and there would be more dead chicks, so then she thought she'd better really keep an eye out on what was happening. She kept looking over at the chicken yard and she said she saw me slip under the fence and then sit in the yard with all these little chicks around me. She didn't think anything of it and she went back to doing her laundry and hanging up her clothes. Then she noticed that when the little baby chicks would come close to me, I would reach out and grab one, then cuddle it against my face. She could tell I really liked how soft they were. I would look at the little chick, laugh, and then I'd throw it.

Grandmother thought, what is she doing? She came closer and noticed that I was grabbing them, and because I liked their soft fuzziness, I would hold them tight. I was squeezing them to death. When their little heads flopped over, she said I'd flop my head over the same way, then toss that one and grab another. Grandmother said, "I had to keep you out of the chicken yard because you liked them too much!"

Grandmother told me that story when my mother told another story about me and baby chicks that happened a few years later, when I was about eight. I lived in L.A. at the time. At Easter time, you could buy one-dollar coupons to go to the local feed store, and with that you got a free chick. The chicks were dipped in food colouring. I saved my pennies for months and went and bought something for a dollar, then got my free chick. Then I had to spend five cents to get food for it. I brought it home and my mother said, "You can't keep a chicken in the house."

I said, "Well, it's just one."

Then she said, "Well, you've got to keep it in your room," so I put it in a shoe box. She told me to put some shredded up newspaper in the bottom. I took a lid from a jar and put water in it and another lid and put food in, thinking the chick would keep it that way. I went to bed that night and all you could hear was, *peep, peep, peep. Peep, peep, peep* all night long—from this little peeping chick.

My mother had finally had enough and she came and said, "You'd better shut that chicken up or it's going to go outside." So, I took it out of the box and as I was holding it, I realized it got quiet. I'd try to set it down and the minute I'd put her down, she'd start peeping again, so I picked her up again. I realize now that the little chick was cold. I didn't know that then. I thought, well, I'll just hold it while I sleep, so I took it to bed with me. When I woke up, I couldn't find it. I sat up and finally found it lying underneath me—a flat, baby chick. I'd killed it. And, so, my mother told my grandmother and my grandmother started laughing and said, "Oh, this girl has something with chickens." And that's why today my partner Pam takes care of the chickens. She won't let me go anywhere near them.

STEAK SANDWICHES

Some of the happiest memories of my life are those from the summers at my grandmother's house. There were unhappy memories too, of course, like when I went to Sunday school there. One of my memories was of Berta and Bertha, the daughters of a German farmer who leased land from my grandparents. They were twins, who came to Sunday school with their matching little lunch boxes. Now, all the Indian kids had lunches that were wrapped in yellow-brown wax paper. Usually, lunch would be a piece of fry bread smeared with beans or maybe potatoes, it'd be rolled up and wrapped in that wax paper, and that's what we had for lunch. If we were lucky we had peanut butter and jelly sandwiches, but not often. Berta and Bertha would come to Sunday school with their little lunch boxes that held Wonder Bread sandwiches. Oh, my eyes used to light up. I used to dream of the day I could have nice, white, fluffy bread for my sandwiches. Today, I know white bread is bad for you and I can't stand it. But in those days, at five years old, that bread looked like it tasted of heaven.

Once, the twins had these big slabs of meat between the bread and my eyes lit up when they took their lunch out. "Are those steak sandwiches?" I asked, and they said, "Yeah." Well, my aunt used to make German chocolate cake—really good German chocolate cake. I had a big slab of that wrapped up in this waxed paper. So, we made a deal. I was never really good at making deals. I tried to trade them half a sandwich for half a piece of cake, but they said no. They wanted the whole piece of cake and they would only give me half a sandwich. I said, "Okay." For about three days, I did that. I knew that I could always get cake at home.

On Saturdays, as usual, we went into town—which was about twenty-five miles away—to do our grocery shopping at the Red Owl Store. Usually by the time we got back, it would be getting towards evening, and we'd stop by the church hall where they would have a pot-luck. Everybody in the community would go and they'd have a social. Sometimes, some of the local boys would come and play barn music, and they'd have a barn dance. The little kids would be playing basketball and just running around like crazy. Some of the men would be playing checkers or cards—or whatever men did. Women would be sitting around knitting, doing bead work, sewing, talking. They'd put blankets on the floor and the smallest kids would lay down and fall asleep.

One Saturday evening, Berta and Bertha walked in. Three women—my aunt, my grandmother and another relative—were sitting near the door. My grandmother said, "Oh, there's the Zaunker's. You know that old horse they had that was thirty years old? It died."

My aunt said, "Yeah, those girls have been going to Sunday school saying that they're eating steak sandwiches."

The other woman, the relative asked, "They were horse sandwiches?"

My aunt said, "Yeah, they butchered that poor old horse. It was nothing but bones, but they butchered it up and they were eating it."

I started screaming, and, of course they asked, "What's the matter?"

"I've been eating horse!" I answered, horrified.

THE OLD SUMMER HOUSE

At my grandmother's, we had a summer house, an old cabin. It didn't really have any windows. There were shutters, but there was no glass in them. It seemed like a huge place to me, but when I go and see its footprint—because the footprint is still there—I see now that it was pretty small. We slept there, but we didn't do any cooking inside the cabin. My grandmother cooked outside all the time.

There was a sweat lodge not too far from there. My grandmother and some other women, one of them being my aunt, often went to the sweat lodge. When I was really little, one of the first times I went to stay with her, I remember they tied a rope around my waist and then they tied the other end of the rope to a tree. My cousin was tied to the other tree, so the two of us kind of waved to each other. I realize now that they did that to keep us safe: tied up like we were, we couldn't get to the fire and we couldn't get to the river behind the lodge. The rope was like our babysitter. They would open the door and ask, "Do you want to come in?" and we'd say, "Uh-uh," and we'd run back as fast as our little legs would allow to the area we could reach and continue playing.

The women built their own fire in the sweat lodge. There was no man there that did that. The women took the rocks inside and then they all went in together. No one took me aside and said, "This is what we're doing, and this is why we're doing it." They just brought me along. There were times when my grandmother would go to someone's house to deliver a baby and I would go with her and watch. There were times when someone died and she would go to help take care of the bodies. I'd go with her and again I'd watch. But she never took me aside and said, "This is what you do."

We used to walk through the forest a lot. She'd be walking along and she'd pick up plants—tasting them, eating them. I still do that, and my kids are afraid that one day I'm going to eat something poisonous and die. That was her way of identifying the plants. But again, she never said, "Okay, this is what this is." Once in a while she'd say, "Taste this." It might be a mint leaf or some chamomile. "That's what I make the tea out of," she'd say. As I said, she wasn't very affectionate, so it wasn't about teaching me, her granddaughter, something, or about sharing her knowledge. She didn't think like that.

The first time I saw a ghost was at that old summer house. My cousin and I were playing outside when we heard a car. You didn't hear cars out there very often, so we thought someone was coming and we were watching. We never saw the car, however, but we heard footsteps on the steps of the old porch going into the log cabin. Then we heard someone knocking. My grandmother opened the door, looked around and asked, "Did you guys knock on the door?"

We said, "No. It was that man." Just before she'd opened the door, we'd looked up and saw a man standing there. The door opened and then he was gone.

She just looked at us then shut the door and went back in.

Another time I was out in the woods, running around and playing. I sat down and started digging in the dirt with a stick, like kids do, and there were beads, little tiny seed beads. I picked them up, very carefully, one at a time until I had gathered maybe a dime size amount in my hand. Of course, I ran back to the house to tell my grandma, "Look what I found!"

She got really upset with me. She said, "You take those back where you found them. Put them back! Exactly where you found them!"

I did. I took them back, and I buried them. When I got home, she had made a tea. She made me stand outside in a big tub while she poured this tea all over me. I think it was cedar tea. She told me that somebody was buried there. For a long time I thought she meant buried under the ground, but later I learned that there was a scaffold in that tree and it was probably pretty old.

On the reservation it took a long time for us to begin adapting to white ways. When you think about it, 1910 was when many of our people started moving onto reservations. When you think about history, that's only about a hundred years ago. That's not a long time when you speak of history, and when you think of all that's transpired over the last hundred years and where Native people are today. My grandmother didn't even have electricity until about 1977. There was no running water either. She had to haul her own water. She still used oil lamps. When she was quite elderly, they made her move into town because they said she was getting too old to live alone.

I went out to the old summer house about twenty years ago. There was hardly anything left of it. It had pretty much collapsed and it had been vandalized. I was amazed that some people would go out of their way to vandalize the cabin, because it was a good seven miles off the main road. And there was nothing there to vandalize really. It was all falling apart. You could hardly tell anybody had ever lived there. She had some lilac bushes, though. Those were still alive. That was amazing to me. I have no idea where she got them or when and how she planted them, but they were in front of her house and they were fully alive. I tried to take a cutting from one of the bushes but it died, and I wasn't able to revive it. I didn't know how to take cuttings in those days. I'd probably be able to do it the right way now.

My grandfather had dug out a big underground root cellar, framed out in timbers that he made from trees that he had cut down. He put tin all around the frame, and in front of that tin he put hay or straw. It wasn't really bales, because it looked like cribs, and he stuffed the hay down in there. Then he put in ice, big chunks of ice that he would cut out of the river during the winter. After he passed, other relatives would come and do that for my grandmother. They would cut these big chunks of ice out of the river, put them on a sled, slide them over there, place them in the root cellar, and pack them all in there. It was an awfully small space, but there were shelves where they could store their vegetables, and other things that needed to be kept cold. During the summer, one of my fondest memories—and to this day, I have no idea where she got lemons—my grandmother would make iced lemonade and iced mint tea. Iced mint tea is still my favourite. I even drink hot mint tea. If I'm drinking tea, nine times out of ten it'll be mint tea.

My grandmother would cut big chunks of ice out for the lemonade and mint tea. She'd send us down with a bucket and an ice pick. There was always a little hammer in there and we'd chunk up the ice and have ice cold drinks in the middle of the summer. It always amazed me that the ice was still frozen, it was so well insulated. Today, we spend a fortune paying for electricity to keep our food cold, but there are other ways that are much simpler. They just take a lot more work.

So, that was my grandmother's old summer house, and as I said, my mom would come and drop me off and then leave. She never really stayed. She wasn't drawn to that place.

MOM AND I VISIT THE OLD SUMMER HOUSE

As an adult, I went back home with my mom and I remember going into the town of Kennel, where my grandmother's summer house was. The town used to be closer to the river, but after the town had been flooded once too often, they put in a big dam and that flooded out the town. They had to move the entire town of Kennel to higher ground, so it was about a couple of miles in from where it originally was. They also had to move the cemetery. They had to dig everybody up and move them and a lot of people say there are still a lot of graves in the original spot that were never moved, and that's why there's one place in Mobridge they claim is haunted. People call the dam bridge there the "Singing Bridge." If you go across that bridge at night, you can hear old men singing. They say it's the spirits of those who didn't get moved. A lot of people back home at Standing Rock wouldn't go across that bridge at night. They were spooked by it.

In that new cemetery, there's a little church with a huge monument dedicated to soldiers who didn't come home. My mother was the only woman on that list, and she didn't die in the war! She lived for many more years. But she never did come home. She talked about how when she went home, people said she thought she was too good for them. She didn't feel like she fit in any more. I could never understand how she felt that way until I grew up and then I began to understand more this dynamic set up by the government to keep Native people apart. The government has destroyed families, destroyed generations, through their policies. I know it's similar in Canada. I'm sure the same things have gone on all over the world where Native peoples are concerned.

We'd go back home for visits, my mother and I. She went back a lot in her last years. My brother would take her back every year, but it was always just for a visit. There was never any intention of going back to stay. She began trying to teach her kids Lakota and was using more Lakota as she got older. I think she realized that she couldn't get away from it, that it was not something that she could just ignore. She was pretty proud of who she was, but at the same time she was also very ashamed; it just depended on what circle she was in. This was probably not a whole lot different from a lot of Native people.

MY OLDER SISTERS, SHARON AND GERALDINE

I learned from my mother that I had two older sisters as an adult. She mentioned that their grandparents were white and she had felt they could raise the girls better than she could. I met my sisters three years after my mother passed, when I'd just turned forty. The truth was that they were raised by a woman named Eunice Burton, who was Cherokee and Black, and they grew up thinking they were Cherokee and Black. When Sher, who is the older of the two—she's four years older than I am—was trying to find some financial help for her daughter to go to Stanford University, they applied for Native funding. Mother Burton told her she was registered on the tribal roles, so thinking they were Cherokee, they flew out to Oklahoma and spent a lot of time in the south going to the different Cherokee tribal offices trying to locate my mother's registration. Of course, they were not able to find any record of her.

Until that time, Sher and her sister hadn't known they were not Mother Burton's biological children. When they came back from their trip, Mother Burton handed them their birth certificates. She had never officially adopted them; she had just taken care of them. She told them that she'd met my mother outside of a social services office. My mother was sitting on a bench crying. She was pregnant and holding Sher in her arms, who was about a year and a half at the time. Mother Burton approached her and my mother said, "I don't have anywhere to go with my children. I have a baby and I'm going to have another one." By then, Mother Burton had already legally adopted a little Chinese American girl. She said, "Well, I'll take her, if you'd like me to, but only until you get on your feet." So, she took Sher. She said at first my mother visited regularly, and that when she gave birth to my sister, Gerry, she brought Gerry to her. Mother Burton took Gerry in as well. For a while after that my mother continued to visit, but then she stopped.

Beverly (on the left), with sisters Geraldine and Sharon, 2002.

My parents had broken up for a while, but eventually they got back together and that's when my mother had me. She'd taken me to Mother Burton as well, but Mother Burton was really sick then and was scheduled for a hysterectomy. She said, "I can't take a really tiny baby now. Come back in about a month, and then I can." But she kept me for a month anyway, and then she needed to have her surgery. My mother had to take me back. She was angry and accused Mother Burton: "You could keep her if you wanted to." Mother Burton simply said, "I can't." So my mother left with me and said she'd come back for Sharon and Geraldine, but she never came back. On my sister Gerry's birth certificate, it lists my father as her father.

After my mother died, I found a letter that indicated that my father might not actually be my biological father. To me, he will always be my father. He's the one who raised me and he's the one who loved me. He was always there for me. Apparently, the sperm donor, as you would have it, was a Lakota man from South Dakota, according to a letter they had exchanged.

I tried to look him up, but he had passed, and I saw no need in burdening the family with that information. So there are a lot of skeletons in my family's closets. People think, well, this is my mom and dad, but we don't know. Sometimes people aren't forthcoming and honest about what their lives were. My sisters Sharon and Geraldine are very angry at my mother. They feel like she threw them away. They have very few nice things to say about her. I listen. I don't agree with all they say, but I respect and honour their anger.

Even well into my adult years, I too felt a sense of abandonment. I could not understand where it came from. At times, I would be in a room full of people, and I'd have to leave. Still today, at times I will find myself floating up in a corner of the room looking down at everybody, myself included. Other times, I have found myself in a strange place when I was supposed to be home in bed, and it's not a dream. When this happens it's vivid and very real. I thought it was an odd sensation. Therapists have told me that when you're a child who's been molested, you often leave your body and go somewhere else. So when you feel frightened or uncomfortable, you disassociate. They have all these fancy words for it. Then they said that the sense of abandonment comes from the abuse.

Yet, after going to therapy and working through some of these things—understanding them even—that sense of abandonment stayed with me. I could not shake it. I always had a fear of being alone. After Mother Burton told me everything, I almost immediately felt a sense of peace. I didn't realize that that's where that sense of abandonment came from—probably from those first three months spent at the hospital because I had been born too early, and then later the month I spent at Mother Burton's. There never was a bond between me and my mother. That explains a lot.

It also explains why for a good part of my life I didn't trust anybody. I didn't know what trust was. I had no touchstone for trust. I realize now that it's because I'd been lied to; from the time I could speak, I had been lied to by my mother. My mother told these elaborate stories. I spent many years trying to find out what was and wasn't real. Was she really in the service? Was she really a student at the University of Kansas? I had to have concrete proof—like her discharge papers, and her transcripts. I had to have tangible proof that what she said was true, and I realized that even in that truth there were probably variations. It took me a while. For a number of years, after I met my sisters, it was very disconcerting, trying to sort out what was my anger at my mother and what was their anger. We had a couple of hard years during that time. Again, thank goodness for therapy that helped me through that, and that helped me integrate myself into a whole person.

My younger sister, Gerry, and I now have a very close relationship. Like my mother, Sharon is sometimes aloof and shows no emotion. But Gerry is the spitting image of my mother— everything she does: her body language, her actions, the way she laughs, the way she grimaces, the way she turns her head, smokes her cigarette, drinks her beer. Gerry's an alcoholic and has smoked all her life. She can be belligerent and ambivalent, and she holds a lot of anger; that was my mother when she was drinking. Part of her resents that I had an opportunity to know our mother and that she didn't. I fully understand that part of it. But it came to the point where I had to tell Gerry, "I love you dearly and I'll always be here for you, but when you're drinking, I need to remove myself from your presence. I cannot be around you. You remind me too much of my mother and it's too painful." When Gerry's sober, she understands. When she's drunk, she forgets. Such is life. She's still my sister.

2.

CHILDHOOD SEXUAL ABUSE

S OME OF MY RELATIVES came up to California during the
Relocation Program of the 1950s, a program the government
set up to get people off the reservations. They would take a
family, put them on a bus or train, and then send them to a big
city. There were several big cities—San Francisco, Detroit, New
York City, Chicago, Phoenix, Denver, Los Angeles. They would
get them a job at some big factory, like Hughes Air Craft, or at
some of the other big factories that were around in those days.
The government would put them up in some run-down hotel for
so many days—a month or so—then they would let them go and
they were supposed to make it on their own in the city. It was
one of the biggest failures the U.S. government ever embarked
upon, because families would come out, they'd spend the month,
and then they'd go back home because being in the city was too
overwhelming.

MY FIRST PAINFUL MEMORIES

Some of my relatives took that opportunity to visit us. Basically,
it was a free vacation for them, and when I was going on six years
old, my aunt and uncle came out. By then, my mother had started
drinking. She was always having people come over. There was
often somebody coming into my room and I'd feel their hands
on my body when I was little. But when my uncle came to visit,
that's the first time that I was aware of being sexually abused
with any certainty. Everything else that had happened before that
had been vague.

Looking back on it now, when I was about two and a half and we still lived in the rooming house, there were two little boys and a little girl that lived next door. We were all playing outside near a big palm tree. One of the boys said that boys were better than girls because they could pee farther. The other little girl—she was about five—said, no that wasn't true, so we had a peeing contest. We put some twigs down on the ground. The boys stood there, dropped their drawers and stuck their little penises out and peed. Well, they got a good stream going. Just about the time I dropped my drawers and was standing there with my hips thrust out ready to pee, my mother walked over. I couldn't sit down for a week. Oh, she really beat me and told me how bad that was and how could I be so dirty? So it was like adding to the humiliation because, you know what? I learned boys really can pee farther than girls. But what I remember most vividly was how mad my mother got.

I was about five years old when my uncle took me to the park. I remembered how angry my mother was so I willingly went with my Uncle Kenny to the park. He said he was going to take me to the park and buy me a soda, and he did. I don't remember much of what lead up to it, and how I ended up with him being on top of me and my skirt lifted. I do remember the pain. I felt like I couldn't breathe. I felt like I was being crushed. I kept trying to push him off and when he finally rolled off he said, "I'm going to tell your mother that I caught you in the bushes with some little boys." Of course, I didn't realize it at the time, but his words had triggered that fear of what had happened when I was two. So I didn't tell my mother. When I got home, I ran into the house and upstairs to the bathroom, put my pajamas on, wadded my clothes up and threw them in the wash. I told her I was really tired and wanted to go to bed. She didn't think it was unusual. Two days later, my uncle left.

My Aunt Viola stayed because she found out she was pregnant. My mom talked her into staying, said she'd take the baby, and that way my aunt would not have to give up the baby for adoption like she'd planned. Ultimately, my aunt got into a fight with my mother and she took off. She went to St. Anne's Home for unwed mothers, gave birth, and then put her baby up for adoption. Then she came back. Mom was really upset with her for giving the baby away. But I guess my aunt figured it would be better to have the baby put up for adoption than to bring the baby to this home where there was all this alcoholism and stuff going on. She'd been there long enough to know that it wouldn't be a healthy place for a baby.

I didn't say anything to my mom about what my uncle had done to me, and for the next few years it seemed like there was always some man coming into my room and doing things to me that I didn't want them to do. I couldn't get them to stop and saying no didn't seem to make any difference. It didn't matter what I did— not even locking my door or pushing furniture up against it made a difference. They always managed to get in. Then I would feel guilty because I thought that I had somehow set myself up for it.

My mother would take off sometimes and go to town. She would tell my dad she was taking me to the movies. I was about seven, eight years old by then. We'd get on the bus and go downtown. When we'd get off the bus, there would be somebody waiting there for her in a car. They would drive me back to our house and send me inside. My mother would tell me to tell my father that she'd be back the next day. Of course, I'd go inside and I'd have to witness my father's anger—not at me, but at my mother. I became afraid for my dad and all his worry, so there were times when my mother was going to go into town and I'd say I wanted to go with her. I'd make up my mind that I wasn't going to leave, that I wasn't going to get out of the car, even if she told me to. So, they'd leave me in the car and my mother and whoever she was with would go to a bar.

I see my growing up as a time when I had to take care of my mom. There were a couple of Indian bars downtown—they called them Indian bars because Indians hung out at them. .I couldn't go inside, but I would sit outside. The bouncers got to know me. One time the police came and tried to arrest me for prostitution and the bouncer, from the Columbine, stepped in and said, "No, she's waiting for her mom. I'll keep an eye on her." So they didn't arrest me. But they thought I was a prostitute, which tells me that I looked a lot older than my seven or eight years old. It was kind of funny, in a gross way.

I was just small enough, just short enough, that I could see things the adults couldn't see. There was this place called the Shrimp Boat. It was nothing more than a metal structure with glass walls where they used to sell deep fried shrimp and pork chops, and other stuff like that, all fried foods. I could see right under the counters because that's about as high as I was and of course, they'd put all the food on top of the counter. I'd be standing there next to my mom and she'd be ordering stuff and I could see them drop shrimp on this grimy, filthy floor and they'd just pick them up off the floor and throw them in the bag to coat them with the batter. My mother would buy the food and I'd never eat it. She never understood why I didn't want to eat.

Then there'd be the times when they'd go down to Huntington Beach and they'd have what they'd call "the forty-nine." It was a pow-wow of sorts. They would use an overturned trash can as a drum and everyone would dance around the drum. Of course everyone was drunk so the dancing was pretty interesting. All these Indians would head down to this beach. Somebody would have a car, and they'd say, "How many Indians can you get in a car?" I'd have to almost take a nose dive into the car so that I didn't lose my mom, if I wanted to travel with her. I was constantly watching, making sure that she didn't disappear on me, and watching them dance around a trash can they'd turned upside down on the beach. It wasn't so much dancing as it was stumbling. Those were the things that I saw.

Another thing I learned at these forty-niners was that there'd always be a group of Navaho people and a group of Lakota people that would get into it. They'd be yelling back and forth, "You dog eaters! You sheep eaters!" It usually wound up with the Navahos being thrown into the ocean by the Lakota's. The Navahos would be okay, but this reinforced the message still, that it was not okay to be a Navaho.

Somewhere during that time, my uncle wrote to my mom and said he was coming out to spend some time with us. I got really upset. I told my mom that I was going to leave. I said, "I don't want to be here if he's coming."

She said, "You haven't seen your uncle for a number of years."

I said, "I just don't want to be here." Every time we'd gone back to South Dakota after he abused me, whenever I saw my uncle coming, I'd run and hide. When he was gone, I'd come out. That's how I discovered all the little mice in the barn. I'd buried myself in the hay and found these little mice nests. Then I'd taken the baby mice, dropped them in a barrel, then put the cat in the barrel, and put the lid on the top. I know. That was really bad, wasn't it?

My mother kept insisting that I be there when my uncle came and finally I told her what he had done. She looked at me and she said, "You've been sleeping around, haven't you? You've probably been pregnant already, and that's probably why you're making this up." I protested, but I realized it wouldn't do any good to protest. That's what she believed. I closed down and I didn't want to talk about it any more. I knew my mother wasn't going to believe me. She didn't believe me any other time, either. When I told her about some friend of hers who came over and I didn't like what he had done to me, she would say, "What are you talking about?" Of course, I didn't even have words for what had happened to me, so I didn't know how to say anything. When she said that to me, I went to a friend's house and I stayed there for four or five days. I didn't return home until I was sure my uncle was gone. I became really quiet. I wasn't an outgoing child at all. I was always very quiet. I kept to myself a lot. I had a few friends, only one or two good friends, so I wasn't the social butterfly type of kid.

When I was ten, we lived with my aunt and the man she married six months after she had given her baby up for adoption. She married and then had a little girl with Steve. She and Steve were living in his uncle's house. The uncle, Joe, lived with his mother. It was a very odd situation. My parents moved into the garage of Joe's house. There was a wood shed next to the garage. My little brother and I slept in there. There was a bed in there and every night, Joe would come into that room during the night. He had these comic books that he got in Mexico, with cartoon characters that you might recognize, like Popeye and Olive Oil, but Popeye had an exaggerated penis and Olive Oil had huge breasts—and they were shown in different sexual positions. He got me interested by saying, "Look at my comic books." Well,

I was at an age when I liked comic books, so I looked. Then he would start saying, "Well, why don't you let me do that? I can do that. Let's imitate the comic book." And he would molest me. This happened almost nightly.

Joe used to like going to the wrestling matches. He'd tell my mother he was going to take me with him. There was this old woman named China that he used to take, too. We'd go pick her up and I'd be sitting in the back seat. When we'd drop China off afterwards, he'd tell me to move up to the front seat. When we were driving, he'd put his arm around me and put his hand over my breast. He pinched me or scratched me because I always tried to get away. My breast was really hurting and I finally told my friend Bonnie what Joe did. Then I said, "That's nothing, this is what he does to me at night."

She said, "That's nasty!"

I said, "I know it is, but I don't know what to do."

Her big thing was, "Well, aren't you afraid you're going to get pregnant?" That had never occurred to me.

Bonnie's mother was a member of the Salvation Army Church and I'd started going there, so that's how we met. I'd joined the choir. They had a Christmas program and we had to have these red dresses. My mother wasn't willing to make me one or to buy one, probably because she couldn't afford it. So, Bonnie's mom, Mrs. Alverado, went out and bought material for my mother to make me a dress so I could be a part of the program. I trusted Bonnie and her mother, and agreed when Bonnie suggested she tell her mother, who went straight to my mother and told her. My mother got mad at me and said, "Now we have to move, because you made those lies up. You'd better get out there and find us a place to live."

So, I did. I walked the streets until I saw a "For Rent" sign and found out how much the house rented for. I returned home and told my mother I'd found a place. We were moved in by that weekend. So, I was really responsible. But my mom never believed me. She never moved a finger to protect me, or even to check out anything I'd said. She just assumed the worst of me. I have to think that she really didn't know how to be a parent.

3.

JUNIOR HIGH AND JUVENILE HALL

THOSE WERE DIFFICULT YEARS, the years that lead to the time I started junior high school. Before the school year started, my mother gave me ten dollars to buy school clothes. I went to a dollar store and I bought two blouses, because they were two for the price of one. They were identical. I bought one bra—mom said I didn't need one, but I felt I did—two pairs of underwear, a pair of socks, a skirt, and a pair of tennis shoes. That was my ten dollars. So I wore the same thing to school every day. I'd come home, wash out a pair of underwear, wash out my bra, and I'd alternate my blouses, but it was always the same skirt. On weekends I'd wash the skirt. The home economics teacher—I think now, looking back at it — meant well. I'm sure that in her mind she was thinking that if this girl's parents couldn't afford to buy her clothes, then she would teach me to make my own. I want to believe that that's what she was thinking. She called me up in front of the whole class and asked, "Do your mother and father work?"

"Yes," I replied.

Then she said, "Then why do you always wear the same clothes to school every day?"

I gave some smartass answer about it being my favourite outfit and that I had so many clothes in the closet, I couldn't make up my mind, so I just wore the same thing every day.

I never went back to that school again. I spent the entire year hanging out at the park. My mom never knew.

It wasn't until the following year that I decided I wanted to go back to school, so I enrolled in another junior high school in our district. My mom never knew that I'd missed that whole year of school. That's how much she paid attention.

At the new junior high, I was always getting called into the principal's office for missing school because on Fridays I had to stay home to clean the house. And if my brother or sister got sick, I had to stay home and take care of them because my mother went to work during the week. On weekends, it was parties and getting drunk for my mom.

Just before my eleventh birthday, my aunt wanted to call an ambulance because her baby was sick. She asked my mom if she could use our phone. My cousin Joyce was about eighteen months old then, maybe two. My mother said no. She was drunk. "It's my phone. You can't use my phone," she said. Drunk people can be so obstinate. My aunt was crying and she was really afraid the baby was going to die. She was very upset. I came out of my room, pushed my mother on the floor, and sat on her. She couldn't get up. I was already bigger than she was. So my aunt made her phone call and then when the ambulance got there, of course my mom acted all concerned. After my aunt left with the ambulance, my mother came into my bedroom, took out her belt and started yelling at me, how dare I disrespect her that way! She started tearing down the pictures I had on the wall of a teen idol, a guy named Paul Anka from Canada. Oh, he was my heartthrob. She started pulling all these pictures off the wall and I went ballistic. She slapped me and I bit her. Then my father came into the room. He was yelling too. He never hit me. Even though my father had never hit me, I was afraid he was going to and I ran out the door.

I ran about five blocks away, and ended up at this woman's house. Her name was Carmon. She saw me coming up the walkway. She saw that my hair was a wreck and she saw that my blouse was torn, and that there was blood, so she called out to her husband, "Ernesto," and said, "Call the police! Beverly's been raped." When I got to the door and she found out that hadn't happened, the police were already on their way. Of course, my mother had called the police and told them I had run away. The officers took me to the police station and they said they were going to arrest me and take me to juvenile hall if I didn't go home with my mother and stop being incorrigible. I didn't want to go home with her because I knew if I went home, there would be more beating, so I said, "No. I'm not going." I reached over, grabbed my mother's hand out of her pocket, and a belt fell out. They finally believed me, so the police took me to juvenile hall.

I liked juvenile hall because they had beds. There was a top sheet and a bottom sheet and both were clean, even if they smelled institutional. They used to put them through those trough mangles with that smell—it was comforting. It was, like, wow, there are sheets here. And a pillow, And a blanket too. Before that, I had slept wherever and on whatever, so going to juvenile hall wasn't the worst thing in the world that happened to me.

When I went in for my physical, though, that was traumatizing. They did a pelvic examination and while I was still laying there with my legs in the stirrups, the nurse looked right at me and asked, "Are you a virgin, young lady?"

I knew that I had been molested and I thought I could tell her, and so I said, "No."

Before I had a chance to say anything else, though, she added, "If you were my daughter, I would have whooped your ass by now." She started berating me because I wasn't a virgin.

I became so angry, I reached out and scratched her, right down her face. She shouted a couple of obscenities and another nurse came over, running. They held me down while they clipped my nails. My nails were clipped so short they were bleeding. For years, I was ashamed of my nails, they were always so short. They never seemed to grow after that. Now I take great pride in going to get my nails done every two weeks. It's something I do for me. I don't know when that shift came, or what healed when that happened, but I learned to love my hands again and I'm glad.

But all that part at the beginning of my stay at juvenile hall was pretty terrifying. Of course, they put me in lock up because I was considered violent. I just cried. I cried for about three days—the whole time I was in there. I didn't understand why the nurse didn't let me explain, why she had simply assumed the worst. They sent me to a psychiatrist. I tried to tell him what had happened, and in his report he told the judge that I had a vivid imagination. So it just felt to me like nobody was listening and nobody cared. That was the message I got. I felt like I had a "Fuck Me" tattoo on my forehead.

Eventually I was sent to a government school called the Sherman Institute, in Riverside. There was a Safeway store and us kids weren't allowed to go in there because kids had shoplifted in the past. There was a big sign on the door that said, "No Indians Allowed." We're talking about the late fifties. Not that long ago. I was there for about six months.

When I was really little, my mom used to bead, and so I learned how to bead. I learned inadvertently. She didn't sit down and teach me. I just bugged her until she showed me. At Sherman, they had a big craft room and I spent a lot of my time in there doing bead work. I learned a lot of different stitches and I learned about colouring, and other stuff like that. After about six months they said they were sending me to another school because only southwestern Indians could go to Sherman. There were some Navahos and Hopis at Sherman. That's one of the only times that I saw that it might be beneficial to be a Navaho.

They transferred me to Stewart, Nevada, which was outside Carson City, for another six months. I had an aunt and uncle living there, my aunt Gloria and her husband, Rudy. Rudy was a teacher and Gloria was a door mom at Stewart, so that wasn't so bad. But then they sent me to Intermountain, in Utah, and I hated it there. Most of the teachers there were Mormon and I was just not going to stay there. So I ran away. I managed to make it all the way back to L.A. hitchhiking. When I think about it now, I know it was a dangerous thing to do. Nobody knew where I was, nobody knew who I was, but somebody else was looking out for me, for sure.

Overall, though, going to boarding school was not a bad experience for me, because by then things had changed a lot. It wasn't as rigid and the churches weren't running them; they had lay teachers. It was interesting because there were kids from all different tribes. But it was very regimented. We had to be up at a certain time, our beds had to be made, and we had to be in the mess hall while our house mothers went through and made sure that things were in order. I kind of liked it because it gave some structure to my life, unlike living with my mother, where I could go out and stay out till two or three in the morning. My mother didn't care. When my friends finished dinner, they had to wash dishes. I didn't. I never had to wash dishes. I had to iron, though. I would iron my father's shirts, and I hate ironing to this day. But I love to wash dishes, probably because I didn't have to when I lived with my parents. But while I was in the boarding schools, there was that structure. You had to be in bed by a certain time and I really enjoyed that. Structure was something that was lacking in my life.

RUNNING AWAY FROM HOME

When I came out of Juvenile Hall, there were many months and weeks in between before I finally went to stay at a convent. It was during one of the summers I ran away from home. I think I was eleven. One of my friends got mad at her mom and said she wanted to run away, and I said, "Okay, let's run away." We left. We just started walking. We walked and walked—it seemed like days, but it was only a few hours and then she decided that we should start hitch-hiking. This man picked us up and asked where we were going and we told him Las Vegas. I don't know why we chose Las Vegas—we were in L.A. The man started driving and when we got to the desert, he turned off onto a side road and said he needed to get out and go to the bathroom. The two of us were sitting in the front seat—I was sitting in the middle. When he got back in, he put his arm around me and he started asking us why we wanted to go to Las Vegas. The way he was talking made me feel uncomfortable. He put his arm over my shoulder and put his hand down on my breast. I had already experienced this with my uncle Joe, and I panicked. I pushed, I pulled, I reached over, opened the door, and pushed Irene onto the ground as I stumbled over her. I grabbed the keys to the car without even realizing it, and I ran. Of course, he came after me. And I ran. He was catching up to me and I just threw the keys as far as I could. It was dark, so it took him some time to find them.

I kept running back the way the car had come. Irene followed me and when she caught up with me, I said, "He could have killed us." She agreed, so we kept running and getting as far away from that car as we could. We made it to the main road and we started walking, and unknowingly—we didn't know anything about directions—we started going back the way we'd come. We saw a car coming and we were afraid it was him, but there was nowhere to hide in the desert. But it wasn't the same man; it was a woman. She gave us a ride and asked us what we were doing out there. We told her that our father's car had broken down and we were trying to get to a gas station. So she took us to a gas station.

At the gas station there was a young man gassing up his car. We asked him how far Las Vegas was and he said, "Well, let's see. You're pretty close to San Bernadino," and we realized we went back the other way. Then he asked us where we lived. Without thinking, I said, "Los Angeles," and he said, "Well, you're going the right way. Are you girls in trouble?" We made excuses, but he knew. Finally he said, "Look. I have a place in the town of Ontario. Why don't you come and you can stay there for the night and then we'll figure out what to do in the morning." So we went with him. The house was empty.

He said he was getting a divorce from his wife and she had taken everything out, but he was still living there. He had no electricity, but he did have running water, and he said we could stay there as long as we wanted. So we stayed. Irene was a little older than I was and she began to have an affair with him. When I say older, I mean Irene was about fourteen.

Then something happened and Irene decided she was going to go home. I was still there and I didn't know what to do. The man was not there all the time, so I was left on my own. I would get up early in the morning, before the sun came up, and follow the milk truck. I would watch the milkman put the milk in these little wire baskets. Sometimes he'd put cottage cheese, sometimes cream. I would steal a bottle of milk or some cottage cheese to eat. There were a lot of grape vineyards. I would go into the vineyards and I would eat grapes. Oftentimes they were green grapes and I would get very, very sick, but it was something to eat. I met some young people and started hanging out with them at a park.

Then the man started wanting me to sleep with him. I wasn't willing to do that, so I left his house and hung out with the kids living in the park for a couple of weeks. This one man—Johnny Colins—was seventeen. He was from Tennessee, and part Native. He took me back to his sister's house, who was married and had two children. He wanted me to marry him. He thought I was sixteen because I told everybody I was sixteen. When I told him I was eleven, he told his sister and his sister called the police. There were several incidents like this throughout my teen years. How I got out of them alive, I don't know.

I was at the police station for about two days, when they finally contacted my mother. They took me back to her and when I walked in, the officer said to her, "We're returning your daughter," and she had to sign some papers. She didn't say, "Hello," She didn't say, "I was worried about you," She just said, "Oh, okay." I wanted to turn around and tell the policeman, "Take me back to jail." At least I was wanted there. They were nice to me there. It was another one of those moments in life when I realized my mom just wasn't going to be there for me. It didn't matter if I was there or not.

THE CONVENT LIFE

When I ran away from Intermountain, I was considered incorrigible because I had done something against the law. After that, the social workers were in my life pretty consistently. I wanted to go to a convent because I thought that would be a good place for me to be. There was a convent in Los Angeles called the Good Shepherd and it was a residential school for girls, so my social worker arranged for me to go there. After a few months, I told Mother Superior that I wanted to become a nun, that's why I had come there. They had what they called a Stair Step, where if you were at school, then the classes that you took kind of geared you towards becoming a nun. I was a Postulant, so to speak, and fully intended to become a nun. I liked the ritual of the mass, and the singing. I was in the choir, although I got chastised a couple of times because I sang louder than everyone else and they said I wasn't blending in. They put me in the back because they felt that my voice carried too far.

What else did I get in trouble for? I got in trouble for riding the other girls on the buffer. We had a big machine buffer. It was a heavy thing. It took two girls to hold it because it would really swing you back and forth. So I got the bright idea that if somebody sat on it, that would keep the machine in one place and make it easier to buff the floor. We'd go down the centre isle of the church with somebody sitting on the buffer and we'd give somebody a ride this way. All the while we buffed the floor and it was fun—until one of the nuns came in and saw us. I was taken off the cleaning crew there and was put on the crew to clean the altar. I don't know if people realize that the host they use in the Catholic Church I don't know if this it's true in Episcopalian churches too—comes in a little packet. I don't know if it comes from Rome and it's been blessed by the Pope and whether that makes it so sacred. The hosts looked like rice wafers to me, like the rice candy you could buy and put in your mouth and that just melted; you didn't even have to take the wrapper off. I always liked the way the host tasted.

When I'd go to communion and they'd put the host in my mouth, I savoured the way it felt and tasted on my tongue. Well, if a host is chipped or broken, they can't use it. Can you imagine a priest standing up there holding a round host with a big chunk out of it? They'd set that one aside in this little box. I don't know what they did with those broken hosts. They weren't consecrated. They weren't holy or sacred. At the time I thought, if the hosts really were the body and blood of Christ, then they would have gotten maggots on them, but they didn't. So, when I was cleaning the altar, I came across this little box. I opened it and I thought, ohhhh, and I had a snack. You would have thought I'd gone up to Christ himself and bit his arm off. Oh, I got chastised for that.

One of our classes was a biology class. It was on the second floor and one day at lunch a bunch of us were in the classroom studying. We heard some giggling. We looked out the window and there was a group of Novices who were preparing as nuns. Postulants wore these black skirts, dark blouses and a sheer veil, but the Novices wore all white. They had the big white collar and a hat. The Novices were outside with the Mother Superior and another couple of the senior Mothers. They were all standing around a big tub, where they had five little kittens—they couldn't have been more than three weeks old—and they systematically drowned each one of them. Then they went over by the rose bush and buried them. We all just stood there and watched them do this. As soon as they walked away—they walked away laughing—we went down and dug up one of kittens. We brought it inside, washed it off, and proceeded to dissect it. They had these boards and you had to pin the carcass open and onto the board. We pinned the kitten open like that and then put it on the teacher's desk. When she came in and saw it, she was horrified. She said, "Who is responsible for this?" I stood up and I said, "I'm responsible for dissecting the cat. You're responsible for killing it." I had to sit in the corner on my knees for hours, and hours, and hours.

One of the sisters had a little dachshund who was so fat that her belly rubbed on the floor. I think the final straw came when I tied two skates to a pillow, put the dog on top of the pillow, and then shoved her down the hall. That's when they told me they didn't think I was cut out for religious life, so my career was effectively ended. But it was a very interesting experience. I never knew that they had a room in the convent that was full of wedding dresses and when you were going to take your first vows you would go in there and choose a wedding dress. They would alter it and make it fit. Then you were given a ring, and you were essentially marrying Christ. They even had an actual wedding ceremony. Then you would go off and come back in your nun's habit, which I thought was very bizarre. There's all this uproar now about two women getting married, or two men getting married. They ought to look at the people in the Church and see who they marry. A virtual marriage, before virtual marriages were even in vogue.

I learned a lot while I was at the Good Shepherd and it was a good experience. And they didn't just kick me out. They arranged for me to go to a different convent that was not cloistered. Cloistered means you stay within the confines of the convent for the rest of your life. The convent they sent me to, interestingly enough, was a Franciscan order, and they were all from Mexico, so all the nuns were Mexican. I thought, that would be nice, and

I guess they thought, well, we'll send her with someone closer to her own kind.

The Mother Superior there was very mean. She would punish the students for any infraction, however minor. The first thing she did was hold my mail because I had spoken back to one of the Sisters. When I was supposed to be praying, I'd whispered something to one of the girls next to me, and so she withheld my mail. The letter that she held was from my mother telling me that they had moved and that right after they'd moved, the house that they'd lived in had burned down because of an electrical fire, and so how lucky it was that they had moved before that had happened.

Well, one day, I had to take the bus to the community where my parents lived to go to a doctor. I took the route that took me by my mother's house—where I thought she lived—and of course when I got there the house was burned to the ground. I was terrified. A friend of mine happened to walk by and she told me my parents had moved.

I said, "Where?" And so she took me to their house.

My mother said, "Didn't you get my letter?" I shook my head, no, I hadn't received it.

When I got back to the convent, I went to Mother Superior and asked for my letter and told her that I'd gone to see my mother, at the wrong house! She was really angry at me and I had to work in the kitchen, on kitchen duty, for I don't know how many weeks.

At the new convent, I was allowed to go home and visit my family on weekends. My mother was not a housekeeper. You had to move stacks of newspaper when you sat down. She did laundry and then she piled it in a great big cardboard box and you had to fish through it to find your clothes. I never had a drawer where I could put my underwear or my T-shirts or anything like that. Everything was just thrown all over the place. So, when I would go home on weekends, I would clean. My father was a smoker also. By the end of the week, he would run out of cigarettes. I learned to collect the long cigarette butts where only one or two puffs had been taken. I'd put them in a coffee can. As I was cleaning, one time I found four unsmoked cigarettes that somebody had dropped out of their pack.

I had this great big tote bag sitting on the couch. I slept on the couch when I went home because there was no place else for me to sleep. I'd tossed the cigarettes into my bag, thinking I'd take them out afterwards, and I forgot. I got back and Mother Superior was waiting. When she asked me to dump my purse that time, she found the four cigarettes, so she made me kneel by the pole, which had a ceramic splash rim all the way around it. It came up in a hump and then kind of came down. I had to kneel there and recite the rosary. I had to be there for four hours and this was at about ten o'clock at night, in February. It was very cold. It was in California, but it was still cold.

After I'd been there about four hours, Mother Superior sent a young nun down to get me. My teeth were chattering and I was shivering, so she took me back up to her room and put me in a warm bath. She began kissing my neck and caressing me. I was crying. I was very upset. She started cradling me and then proceeded to sexually molest me. I was in shock. It wasn't that I didn't know that women could be together. In juvenile hall there were women who were together. When I was first at juvenile hall, at about te years old, a girl named Alexandra asked me if I wanted to go with her, and I thought she meant do you want to be my partner because we had to go everywhere in twos, so I said, "Yes." Then that night, when I went to bed, she leaned over from her bed to kiss me goodnight and I screamed bloody murder. We both wound up in lock-up. I was transferred to another room and she was transferred somewhere else, but that was about as much as I knew about that.

That night, I went back to my room and wondered, well, was that okay? After that night, she treated me like I didn't exist. I guess I began to act out, and I ran away. I was picked up and put back in juvenile hall. They were talking about putting me in a girls' reformatory, and I said, "No, I don't want to go to a reformatory."

They said, "You don't have a choice."

I had heard about a place called David Margaret, an orphanage for children. I said, "That's where I want to go."

They said, "Oh no, that's just for kids who don't have parents."

I said, "Well, I don't have parents who want me." After a

couple of weeks my social worker made arrangements for me to go to David Margaret.

So I wound up in this Methodist home for children. They assumed I was Catholic because I'd come from a convent, so they let me go to mass in the community. I liked it at the home. They had horses and cows and rabbits. It was like a farm. Each girl had her own little cubicle. I felt like I was thriving there. I started school in the ninth grade, I was getting good grades, I was active in the choir and the drama club –doing things that normal kids do. Then my social worker came one day and said, "I am transferring, so you're going to get a new social worker and I don't know if she'll approve you still being here," and from that point on, I felt fearful.

The new social worker came and the first thing she said to me was, "Well, we know your mom and dad don't want you, and we know that you have been in the system, so I'm going to petition the court to make you a full ward of the court to be put up for adoption."

I said, "Who says my mom and dad don't love me?" I knew my father loved me but I couldn't say that my mother loved me. But I fought. I started doing everything I could to get into trouble. Within a month, they agreed to send me home, and on a Friday evening, they drove me to East Los Angles. No one was home, so they put my shopping bags with my belongings on the porch and I sat on the porch until my mother came home. She came up the stairs, she looked at me and she said, "Oh, you're back." I thought, maybe if I'm good she'll want me to stay here. That first night I was back she got drunk. In the middle of the night I had to leave the house and I slept outside on the porch.

I went to school and that was my first semester of the tenth grade. I got straight As and one F. It wasn't because I didn't try, it's just because I couldn't grasp the concept of algebra. I did all my homework, I did all my tests, I did extra-curricular work, but I just couldn't get algebra. The teacher helped me and he said, "I still have to give you an F." So, here I had this report card with straight As and one F. When I showed it to my mother, the F was the only thing she saw. I was totally and completely deflated.

DRESSES AND RUFFLES AND TINY TEARS

Even though I was totally deflated, a couple of things came to mind that were significant in my childhood concerning my mother. I so wanted my mom to be available, and there were times when she actually was. I remember very vividly, one Easter my mother had gone out and bought fabric to make Easter dresses for my sister and I. Mine was very dark. Dark teal. My sister's was pink, a very pretty pink. I wanted the pink but my mother told me the blue was for me. We used to go to a Nazarene church that was run by a Navaho man and his wife. She came by on Saturday to check on us and reminded us that the next day was Easter. She told us that they were going to have an Easter egg hunt and to make sure we were ready when the bus came.

I was very excited so I said to her, "We're going to have new dresses to wear tomorrow 'cause it's Easter."

She said, "Oh, did your mom buy you new dresses?"

I said, "No, she's going to make them."

She said, "She's going to make them?"

And I said, "Yeah," and I showed her the fabric sitting on the table.

She said, "Oh, she hasn't started them yet."

I said, "No, she says she's going to make them today."

She patted me on the shoulder and said, "Sweetheart, it doesn't matter. God doesn't care what you wear to church tomorrow. You just come. Even if it's an old dress, you wear it and you come. The important thing is that you're there." I was baffled because she didn't believe my mother was going to make the dresses. But I was certain that my mother would have them ready.

The next morning I woke up, and the dresses were done. Oh, they were beautiful. They were quite intricate. They had tooling and little flowers that were sewn onto them, they were gathered and picked up around the sides and they had lace all around the collar. And she made petticoats. When I walked into church, Mrs. Begay was so surprised that we both had our dresses. So there were times when my mom did follow through and I think that throughout my childhood there was always that hope that maybe this time it would last.

My mother was a good seamstress and most of our clothes were made by her. One time she made me a dress—and again it was that same blue, but a blue plaid this time. It had a little white apron over it, with ruffles. The bottom of the dress had ruffles and it had this big sash around the waist, and little puffy sleeves. Very girly. It also had a petticoat. When I was little, petticoats were the thing. They'd wash them in sugar and dry them in sugar so they'd stiffen. My mother had me try on this dress and I was bouncing around because when I walked the dress and petticoat bounced. I felt like a little princess. I said, "Can I go show my friend?"

She said, "Okay, but don't get it dirty."

I ran out the door and there was a chain-link fence, maybe two and a half feet tall, that was put up between two buildings to stop people from cutting through. As kids, we used to jump the fence all the time. So, I ran outside, saw the fence coming up, put my hands out, and threw my legs up to catapult over it. I kept running, but my ruffle was caught on the fence. I must have gone half a block, but my ruffle stayed on the fence. The entire ruffle had been ripped from the bottom of the dress. My mother was so mad. I guess it took a long time for her to get that ruffle just right. It's no wonder that she always chose dark colours for me because she must have been afraid I'd get them dirty. I wasn't the girly-girl type. I preferred to be in jeans and T-shirts at a time when little girls didn't wear those things.

When I was very young—maybe three—my mother asked my father to take me down to Sears to buy me a pair of shoes. We took the bus to the store and when we were looking at the shoes, I spotted a pair of little red cowboy boots. Those were the shoes I wanted, so my dad bought them for me. We came home, and my mother was so mad! She said, "She can't wear cowboy boots all over the place!" I didn't want to take them off and my father finally said, "Oh, let her have them." I wore those boots till I couldn't get my feet in them any more.

My dad would always buy me things. He bought me an airplane, a big metal airplane. He bought me a fire engine too. My mom wanted me to play with girly things, but I never owned a doll. I was never given a doll when I was growing up. I do remember when I was five, almost six—we lived at the house in the projects—and Tiny Tears, the doll, had just come on the market. It was a doll you could give a bottle to and tears would come out of its eyes and then it would wet its diaper. I really wanted one, and at Christmas, when we went to the department store to see Santa—because that's where he lived when he wasn't at the North Pole, so we were told—I very loudly said, "I want a Tiny Tears doll. That's all I want for Christmas."

As we were going through the department store, my mother would make me sit by one of the columns with my little sister and brother and babysit them while she did the shopping, and I saw her pick up a Tiny Tears doll. I was so excited. I thought, oh, I'm going to get my Tiny Tears doll. Then at Christmas, I opened my box and instead of a Tiny Tears doll there was a Mickey Mouse watch. My sister got the Tiny Tears doll. I was crushed. But, I smiled and said, "Oh, I always wanted a Mickey Mouse watch." On my way to school after vacation was over, I threw the watch in the creek. I told my mother that I lost it. She was mad, but at least I didn't have to look at that ugly old watch. Now, in retrospect, if I still had that watch today, it'd be worth a ton of money. But I left it in the creek, so some frog enjoyed it.

A few months after Christmas I was playing outside in the mud and under the oleander bushes when I found the Tiny Tears doll. My sister had left it there and it had been rained on. I carefully took it out of the mud, and up to the bathroom sink where I washed her, cleaned her all up, got some scraps of fabric from my mother's sewing box and made some doll clothes. I probably just wrapped the fabric around her and cut little arms in it or something. I was playing with her. Well, when my sister saw me, she wanted her doll back and I remember crying and telling my mother, "But she abandoned her. She wasn't good to her baby. She left her underneath the bush." My mother said, "Well, that's still her doll," and I had to give it back to her. I was so angry, because I felt like that was unfair. That is the only memory I have of playing with a doll. I did have lots of paper dolls. I would sit and cut them out of scraps and play with them. But, I never had a real doll.

I never had any stuffed animals either. My first stuffed animal was given to me by Elisabeth Kubler-Ross, a doctor who wrote a lot of books on death and dying. She was given credit for being one of the leading, cutting-edge researchers on the study of death and dying. I mentioned to her during a session I had with her that I'd never had a doll or a stuffed animal and she, and the therapist I was working with, went out and bought me a little stuffed bear, which I still have. Yup, my mom wanted a little girl and she got me. I guess she's lucky I only pulled the ruffles out of one dress.

4.

MY EARLY MARRIAGES

WHEN I WAS FIFTEEN, I started dating Joe, who was the same age as I was. When he drove me home, we used to park in the driveway and sit in his car with the windows rolled down. In those days, they used to have these small record players that you could plug into the car. We had three records, and we'd listen to the same three records over and over again. One night, my mother stumbled out of the house. She was really drunk. She walked over to my side of the car and started hitting me through the window. She called me a slut and a whore and then she started yelling at Joe. She said, "If you got her pregnant, you'd better think about marrying her. I'm not having any bastard grandkids." I was so embarrassed. Joe just started the car up, backed up, and we split.

Joe took me to his mother's house. His mother made me sleep in her bedroom with her, and not with Joe. I lived there for about three weeks when his mother said to him, "You two have to get married because it doesn't look good with her living here." So, we went to get a license but I was told I would have to get my mother's permission and signature. When I went to see my mother, she agreed to sign. She didn't care, she'd sign. When we went back to get permission from the judge, he said, "Well, are you pregnant?"

I said, "No, we have never had that kind of sex."

He asked, "So why are you getting married, then?"

I remember my answer was, "Well, because I love him?" The judge just shook his head. He signed, and we got married. But it was a doomed relationship from the start. We were both too young and it was a mating that happened for all the wrong reasons. Joe was a gang member and eventually he was shot and blinded. I have no idea where he is today. But at the time, I felt that being married to him was better than living with my mom.

THE BIRTH OF MY FIVE CHILDREN

The first three nights we were together, Joe and I barely knew what to do. It took us three nights to figure it out, but it wasn't long before my son Rick was born. Rick was premature. When he was born, my mom stood outside the room. When the doctor walked away she took the chart and after scanning it for a moment, she said, "Oh, the doctor says it's a preemie." It wasn't until that moment that I realized she had been convinced I was pregnant when I got married. It was a hard time. I never got any positive stuff from my mom in that respect. And being married was not at all what I thought it would be. I got to buy my white bread and eat it, but my husband, being the same age as I was, couldn't get a job. I tried to go back to school but I was not allowed to. Nowadays if you're pregnant, you can still go to school and they even have parenting classes to help you. Those days, if you were pregnant, you weren't allowed to go to school. If you were married, you couldn't go to school either. They didn't want you mingling with the innocents because you were considered knowledgeable after marriage. Half the kids in school were having sex. It was ludicrous. I tried to get through the eleventh grade, but I wasn't able to and eventually I had to drop out because of the pregnancy. I wanted to graduate. It was important to me, but not to my husband. He dropped out of school too. It didn't matter to him.

After Rick was born, I tried to go back to school for quite a while, and finally got admitted to a class at a hospital where I could train to be a nursing assistant. I took the ten-week course and got a stipend whenever I went. During that time, Joe got arrested for raping a woman. I don't know if he did or not; the woman dropped the charges. It was a big shock to me, and the beginning of the downfall of our relationship because I didn't know if I could trust him anymore. I left for a time and lived with my son alone in a little apartment, but I couldn't afford childcare, so I wound up taking my son to his grandmother, Joe's mother, and asking her if she would take care of him. Meanwhile, I applied and got accepted into a nursing program. I had to go through another ten weeks of nursing assistance classes, and then I was finally admitted into the program and could start to work toward my LPN, my nursing license. They told us the day we started class that if anybody got pregnant during the fourteen-month program, they would be dropped immediately. I thought if I got straight A's and did my very best, they wouldn't kick me out. Six months later it was obvious that I was pregnant, and I got kicked out. So I thought, well, I'll try this again later.

Then I had my son, Gary. I never really knew whether Gary was my husband Joe's son, or my friend Armando's, because Armando and I got together one night when both of us were drunk. He called the next day and said, "Do you remember what happened?" I didn't, but the result was Gary, whose birth spoke volumes about what happened that night. Armando and I were just really good friends, so there was no talk of marriage and no talk of a blended family, so when Gary was born I gave him my husband's name because I truly wasn't sure. Gary was much older when I told him that his dad was probably not the same as Rick's. Anyway, by the time Gary was a few months old, I was divorced and I had two children to take care of.

My good friend Armando was the sponsor of a car club and I started going to his car club meetings and hanging out with the people there. At the time, I had a car that was all decked out. At the same time, the American Indian Movement—AIM—was beginning to form in California, so I started attending some of the rallies and some of the meetings, mostly just watching on the periphery. Then, when Gary was nine months old, I met a man at one of the rallies who said he was part Apache, part Hispanic and part Hawaiian, which I thought was an odd combination. Caesar was very good to my children. I was determined that just because I was a divorced woman, I was not going to be loose, so I had thrown away my birth control. I had told myself I wasn't going to have sex. I was becoming very moral. Caesar had a

twenty-one day leave from the service—he was in the Marines—
and he was getting ready to go to Vietnam. He had volunteered
to go. One thing led to another. He departed on May 7th and on
May 21st I sent him a letter saying he was going to be a father.
I had thought about giving the baby up for adoption, but in
my seventh month I thought, what if it's a little girl? I wanted a
daughter. Again, just before this happened, I had been accepted
into a nursing program at the local university and again, because
I was pregnant, I was dropped from the program. Then I thought,
well, maybe it's just not meant for me to become a nurse. Caesar
was in Vietnam, and I gave birth to my beautiful Gina. When
Caesar came back from Vietnam, he wanted to be a family and
we got married. He wanted a big family, so I got pregnant again
and had Alexx. But by the time Alexx came along, the marriage
was not working as well as I had hoped. We were fighting a lot
and I was very unhappy.

Too, at that point, there were women in my life that I admired
and I really looked forward to being around these women. I began
to question myself. At night I would tell Caesar I was going to
the store and instead I would drive to a local bar called the Plush
Pony—this was in Los Angeles. It was a gay bar. There were lots
of women in there. A lot of the women sat at the bar and when
I walked in they turned their heads to look at me. I felt like they
were undressing me and I thought, I don't fit in here. So I turned
around and walked out. I thought, that's not what I'm like. I can't
relate to that, so I must not be gay.

Then I got pregnant with Lushanya. This time, I wanted to
abort the baby. I didn't want another child. When I went to
inquire about the possibility of having an abortion, I was told
that I couldn't have one because my husband, as the legal father,
had to sign a consent form. I was very upset and cried all the
way home. When I got further along in my pregnancy, I accepted
it, and told myself well, this one will be the last.

When my labour started, I didn't experience any pain. I had
gone to see the doctor in the morning and had asked, "How long
until this baby's born?"

He'd said, "Well, you can't walk around like this forever,"
which was really no answer.

I went shopping and while I was shopping I started leaking water. I ignored it, hoping the contractions would start. I went home, I fixed dinner. No contractions. I mopped the floor, I gave the kids a bath, and then I had a bloody show. I thought, oh dear, so I called the doctor and the nurse said, "Get into the hospital immediately." I thought, yeah right, I'm not having any labor pains. So I proceeded to do some more laundry, do some cleaning, pack a bag, take a shower and finally at ten o'clock, the nurse called me and said, "Where are you?"

My husband and I drove to the hospital and I said, "I feel silly going in there. I'm not in any pain." But we went in and they put me on a monitor right away. The nurse said, "Oh, you're going to have a little boy."

I said, "What?"

She said, "The heart rate shows a little boy."

I said, "No, I want a girl."

She said, "Well, it doesn't really matter as long as it's healthy, right?"

And I said, "No, I want a girl."

She tried to pacify me and finally I locked myself in the bathroom, sat on the floor with my back against the door, and cried. I planted my feet so that I couldn't move. They finally convinced me to come out. I said, "If it's a boy, I don't want to have it tonight, I'll wait till tomorrow. If it's a boy I've got to go home and get used to this idea." It was horrible. But I got into the bed. It was 11:46 p.m. Then, I started having contractions a minute apart. That's how they hit. Not five minutes apart, not ten minutes apart—suddenly, every minute.

They brought me into the delivery room and I was screaming for them to give me something for the pain. "Knock me out! I don't want to feel it," I yelled.

The doctor said, "Beverly, it's a girl." I cursed him out, called him a liar.

The nurse said, "No, Beverly, it's a girl, look." Other people chimed in.

I opened one eye, and I said, "It's a girl! I'm so happy!" Lushanya was a little angel. I was thrilled. This was the child that I was going to abort. She continues to surprise me in so many ways since she's grown up. I love her to death and I'm so glad I gave her a chance.

Two weeks after Lushanya was born Caesar said, "I don't want to be married any more. I don't want five kids," and he walked out. I found out he'd been seeing his secretary the entire year before and I was devastated. I fell to pieces. What was I going to do with five kids? How was I going to make it through with five children? I thought, I just can't do this. But they're all grown now and on their own. None of them is starving, so I guess I did a pretty good job.

It was really rough for a while. I'd buy a bottle of alcohol and drink it. I hooked up with one of my cousins who smoked a lot of marijuana. I started smoking a lot of pot, which goes hand in hand with alcohol. I had a joint in one hand and a drink in the other. Why I never got caught or stopped, I have no idea.

But I had also started to follow my Native ways and was already going to the sweats in California, which Caesar didn't like. At the sweats, they talked about living your life in a good way and I had to say, I wasn't, so I started looking at my life. When Caesar finally left for good—because he came back and forth and I never knew when he was going to return or how long he was going to stay—when he finally left for good, I had the locks changed.

A STROLL THROUGH ODD FELLOWS CEMETERY

There were many times after I'd gotten married that I would go and spend the night at my mom's because things were not good with my husband. My mom would get drunk and then kick me out so I would go across the street to an old cemetery called Odd Fellows. It was a Jewish cemetery. I would squeeze through the fence with a blanket and sleep under the oleander bushes until morning and when I'd wake up, I'd wander through the cemetery looking at the head stones. The head stones had small photographs in them, photographs of the people who had died. They fascinated me. I would stand there and look at the photo, then at the ground, and think, wow, that's who's underneath all this dirt. To this day, one of my favorite pastimes is to stroll through an old cemetery looking for headstones that have photographs. I guess that's why

I'm very comfortable at cemeteries and death doesn't bother me. I'm not afraid of dead people.

MY FIRST ADULT SWEAT LODGE EXPERIENCES

In the early 1970s, the sweat lodges were run by men, for men. The focus was on suffering, and healing. A man would go into a lodge and burn his shoulders. He suffered there and then purified himself. But as a woman, I couldn't suffer enough. Yet, I continued to go into the sweat lodge over at an Elder named Ernie Peters. How I got there is interesting. A man named John approached me one day and said, "We have several case loads of Christmas cards that we didn't sell and I thought maybe you'd like to buy them." They were Christmas cards with pictures of the holy family on them.

I said, "Why would I want to buy those?"

He said, "Well, you're Christian, aren't you?"

And I said, "I never said I was Christian. How dare you!"

He said, "Well, I never see you at the Lakota lodge."

I said, "I can't afford to go back to South Dakota every week."

His response was, "Well, Ernie Peters runs a lodge. He's Paiute and he runs a lodge over at Chuck Salazar's house." He wrote down the directions and phone number and added, "Here. Come on a Friday around six. Just bring a potluck and a large sheet or something to wrap yourself up in."

I said, "Fine. I'll be there."

So, I went home and I called my mother. "Mom," I said, "is a sweat lodge that place where Aunt Viola and Grandma used to go? What did they do in there? I know it was hot, but what did they do?"

She said, "Oh, everybody goes in there and they sit on the ground naked in a circle and the leader pours water on the rocks." All I heard was everybody sits around the circle naked. John was about twenty-four. Most of the guys I knew would be there were in their early twenties. The idea of sitting naked in front of all these men was not my idea of fun. I hung up the phone and I thought, oh, what have I gotten myself into? So I made something for the potluck, found a sheet, got in my car and drove past Chuck's house where I saw some cars parked. I drove on till I got to a strip mall and decided to do some shopping. I called Chuck and said, "I'm sorry, I'm lost. It's now seven-thirty. Must be too late." He said, "Oh, don't worry about that. We haven't started yet." He gave me directions again, and this time I drove to a Jack in the Box, a fast food place, had some dinner, and read the paper. At a quarter to nine I called him again. "I am totally lost. I'm way out here in Diamond Bar."

He told me to get back on the freeway and get off at this certain exit. "Stay there and I'll come and pick you up," he said.

I said, "No, I'll find it, I'll find it." I was only about two blocks away.

I got back in my car and thought, well, I'll drive by the house because I have to go that way to get to the freeway. I decided that I would go home and that I wouldn't call again. But when I drove by the house, Chuck was standing in the middle of the road. "Beverly, I knew you could find it!" He had me. So, I parked and got out of the car and walked into the house. There were a lot of women sitting around. Chuck was a hoarder. He and his wife had piles up to the ceiling of all kinds of things, so you had to move stuff around to find a place to sit. The kitchen was full of dirty dishes, so I put my potluck down on the stove and immediately started cleaning the kitchen. The TV was blaring, but nobody was really listening. Kids were running all over the place. There were sliding patio doors that led outside and I could see a wooden fence about four feet tall. All I could see behind that fence were a bunch of men. I could only see them from their chests up. They didn't have shirts on, so I figured they must be out there naked. I thought, oh my, now what do I do? So, I washed dishes. When the dishes were done, I sat down. A woman named Ruby was sitting near me and she said, "Oh, I'm so glad you came." We chitchatted about what was going on at the Indian Education Commission, which was where I was working at the time.

All of a sudden I heard singing. I looked out the sliding doors and I could see the top of the lodge and one man standing outside the lodge but nobody else. I could hear the singing and I thought, ah, they didn't know I was here so they went ahead and started without me. Oh well. At about eleven-fifty, just before midnight, Chuck walked in with a towel wrapped around his waist and he said, "Okay, they're ready for the women." I was thinking about telling him that I was going home. But then Ruby said, "Come on, we'll go up to the front bedroom. That's where the women change."

I said, "Oh."

She said, "You did bring a sheet or something, didn't you?"

I said, "Yeah."

She said, "Oh, that's big. I'll help you put it on so you don't trip over it."

"Oh, so we wrap ourselves up in our towels or sheets?" I asked.

She said, "Yeah, you didn't think we went out there naked, did you?"

I shook my head, "Of course not. Oh no, no, no."

So we changed, walked through the house and out to the lodge. All the men had come out of the lodge and gone into the house. There was only one man standing there, the man who was going to pour the water over the stone. He saw me and said, "Oh, I'm really glad that you're here." He was my cousin, Archie. We entered the sweat lodge and I simply copied whatever the woman in front of me was doing. Nobody instructed me. Nobody told me what to do.

The ground was muddy and wet, and there were little indentations in the earth that had bits of water in them. My hand hit one of these indentations and I thought, eewwww, some man's sweat, and I shook the water off my hand. I was like a cat who's gotten wet and is shaking the water off. I wound up right in the seat of honour, directly across from the door. It was dark and I could only watch everything that was being done through the glow of the fire. The man brought in these stones that were glowing red. I was terrified. He shut the door and the whole lodge was filled with this eerie light. He started pouring water and singing. The guy liked to sing. He sang and he sang and he sang. I thought, I'm going to die. It's so hot in here, I'm going to die. But at the same time, I felt like I had come home.

When I was growing up there were periods of time when we would go to revival meetings at different churches. We'd go and join these big calls to the Lord. People would go up to the front, kneel, and accept the Lord as their saviour. They would make a commitment and Jesus would save them. I was probably saved about a dozen times. Afterwards, they'd always give you Kool-Aid and cookies, so I was always there. I was baptized Presbyterian. I was baptized Methodist. I was baptized Jehovah's Witness and I was baptized Catholic. The only religion I missed was the Jewish religion, I think. They always told me that the Lord would come and touch me when I was saved. I would know it because I would feel Jesus touch me. I never felt anything, so I used to think, well, with the words "Fuck Me" tattooed on my forehead, no wonder, not even God wants me, and really gave it no more thought.

Until that night, that is. The night I found myself sitting on that ground, in the mud, wetness seeping through my sheet, feeling grossed out because I was sure it was somebody's sweat, sure that somebody could sweat that much—and feeling like I might not make it out alive—was the night I felt Spirit touch me. I knew I had come home. I knew that's where I belonged. I knew that I would never leave that space. And still today, it is to me the safest place in the world that I know. It is the place that I want to be when things are falling in around my head. When I feel like I can't even take another step. During the ceremony the lodge is covered with blankets to hold the heat inside. Even when the blankets aren't on that lodge, I want to go and sit and just be held there because I feel like all my ancestors are there.

I left there in in total awe, wanting to know more, really wanting to know more. I started going every Friday night, which caused great difficulties in my marriage to Caesar. Then our marriage split up and for that whole year, while going to the lodge, I was still using. I was drinking and using marijuana. Finally, I realized that this was a contradiction and so I vowed to stop the drugs. The alcohol was a little different. I didn't see that as a problem. I didn't see myself as an alcoholic because I didn't act like my mother.

I got mad at my cousin one day. We were drinking and I had bought a couple of six-packs of beer, so I picked up one of the six-packs and told her, "I'm going home." I walked out the door with this beer in my hand and I walked past this church. All these people were milling around outside, talking and smoking cigarettes. Jovially, I said, "What's going on, a party?"

They said, "Well, no, it's an AA meeting."

I said, "Well, I have triple A." (That's the Automobile Club of America in the United States.)

They said, "No, no, Alcoholics Anonymous."

And I said, "Well, I'm an anonymous alcoholic." I was just drunk enough to be obnoxious.

Then a woman named Barbara asked me if I would stay, if I wanted to? I said, "Sure."

She said, "Well, let's go get you some coffee."

I said, "Well I don't want to throw away my beer. I want to take it in with me."

She said, "No, no, let's leave it outside." So she helped me find a safe place to put it.

Then we went inside. She got me coffee and we walked right up to the front and sat down. It was the kind of church that has three sections. It had two aisles and we were right in the middle. They started their meeting and it wasn't too far into the meeting that I thought, holy shit, these people are serious. They really see themselves as alcoholics and acknowledge that alcohol has played a big part in their lives. What am I doing here? I don't have that problem. I couldn't leave because we were sitting in the front and I was too embarrassed to walk out. I knew I was tipsy and I was afraid I'd stagger on my way out. So when it was over, I went outside. Barbara followed me and said, "Let me give you a ride home."

I said, "Oh, no, no, I only live about eight blocks from here,"

But she insisted and said again, "Let me give you a ride home." So, we got into her car and she asked, "Are you hungry?"

And I said, "A little bit."

We stopped at a diner and she bought me dinner. Then she talked to me a little bit about her experience with AA. Then she took me home. Somehow she got my phone number and a couple of days later she called and asked if I wanted to go to a meeting. I said, "Oh, no, I have five kids. I can't just up and go like that."

She said, "That's okay, I understand." But she called me every day for a week. Finally, she called and said she found a babysitter for me, that her daughter was willing to come over and stay with the kids while we went to the meeting.

I thought, oh, great, now what do I do?

After two weeks I finally agreed to go to a meeting with her. While I was sober, I listened to what they said. I listened to the twelve traditions and I thought, you know, I'm fast on my way to becoming an alcoholic. I'm going to hit bottom. My parents were alcoholics and I'm a result of that and I don't want to be like my mother and father. So I went to the AA meetings, and going to the lodge also reinforced that drinking was not okay. I saw men going to the lodge, pretending to be holier than thou, when the week before they'd been out somewhere, completely smashed.

Going to the lodge made a profound difference in my life.

ME, LOIS AND ANNA MAE AQUASH

The American Indian Movement (AIM), was just forming in California, just about the time Anna Mae Aquash, who was Mi'kmaq, came out our way somewhere in 1975. Three of us— myself, another woman named Lois, and Anna Mae—went into a lodge and we were all just sitting there. We started talking about spirits and wondering whether our grandmother spirit was with us in the lodge and if she could see everything we did? How about when you're making love, can she see you then? we asked. Then, "If one of us dies before the other, how will we let the others know we are visiting in the lodge?" This was the kind of talk we were having.

Lois said, "Well, when I die, you're going to know I'm in the lodge because I'm going to be that water that bounces off a rock and hits you on the leg to wake you up."

I said, "Well, I'm going to be that little chip of rock that comes off the big rock and hits you."

Anna Mae said, "Not me. When I die, I'm going to be the rain. I'm going to be the rain and when you hear the rain on top of the lodge you'll always remember that it's me." And I always have remembered those words. Every time I am in the lodge and it rains, I tell that story.

It was only a few months later that Anna Mae was found dead. I always felt a Native person killed her, so when they said it was the FBI, I rejected that. I said, no, and I told some people that I didn't believe the FBI, was responsible. I believe that it was some of our own people. I made enemies of several people because of my stance. Then a couple of years ago, they found out that it was in fact two Native men who killed her, Native men who were a part of AIM.

5.

THE AMERICAN INDIAN MOVEMENT

ERNIE PETERS WAS A MEDICINE MAN who lived in Los Angeles and was married to a woman named Teresa. They had four children. Apparently, he'd been in the service and he began getting involved with AIM when AIM was first established. He organized a group of Native men in the Los Angeles area called the West Coast Chapter. Ernie was also running sweat lodges. He was very controlling. When I started going to the lodges at Chuck Salazar's house, Ernie Peters was pouring the water. Women would come and we would wait while they ran sometimes two or three lodges, and at about midnight—sometimes later—they would come into the house and say it's time for the women to go to the lodge. After about a month and a half of this, and listening to him talk about how, as women, it was important for us to teach our children our language and traditions, and take them to the lodges, I couldn't help but say, "Well, if that's important to us as women, then why do we have to wait till after all the men are done? It's much easier to get children to go in the lodge when they're awake than in the middle of the night when they're asleep." He just glared at me.

MEN'S SWEATLODGE TEACHINGS

One day, I had the courage to say, "Ernie, have you ever considered teaching a woman how to pour water so that maybe we could put up two lodges, one for the men and one for the women? Because my mom said to me that back home men and women always had their own lodges. They were always separate." When I said, "My mom said," again, he interrupted me with, "Well I don't see your mom here at the sweat, and, no, I'm not going to teach a woman how to pour water. You've been listening to too many bra-burning women's libbers." He said this in front of everybody and I felt ridiculed and humiliated. He basically said, if you don't like this, then don't come.

That didn't stop me from going, but a few months later I gathered up the courage to bring it up once again, and I said, "Maybe if we built a bigger lodge, then more men could sweat at one time and the women could get in earlier, because with children it's very hard to wake them up at midnight or later and get them into the lodges." I was again met with derision. They thought I was arrogant, an uppity woman who was on a quest for power. I said, "I don't care if it's me you teach to pour—even if it's another man who pours—just that women have another lodge for our children. How can we teach our children if you don't teach someone else?" He was having none of it. After that, every opportunity he got, he would challenge me or try to showcase something I'd done wrong or unknowingly.

One time Leonard Peltier was in California at Lompoc—we'd been going up there to see him—and when he escaped, we all mobilized to find him before the police found him, to try to get him out of the country. There was someone who was prepared to fly him out of the country, but we couldn't find him. Peltier was hiding out in the countryside. We had twelve nights of sweats. Every night we would go down to the lodge and one of the medicine men, Leonard Crow Dog, said that we should start giving flesh offerings each night for Leonard Peltier. I didn't know what flesh offerings were. At Sundance, they would take flesh offerings, but I was usually in the kitchen cooking, so I was never there during that part of the ceremony.

They lined us up and when I got up to the front of the line, I asked, "Could you explain the meaning of the flesh offering again to me?"

Ernie Peters just stopped and looked at me with a scowl, and said, "Well, if you don't know what the meaning of this is, then you probably shouldn't be up here giving it."

I said, "Well, I just want to know why I'm doing this. I just want an explanation of what the meaning is behind it."

He said, "Well, if you're not doing it for the right reasons, Spirit will let you know. Spirit will strike you down."

So lightening was going to strike me down, or a ball of fire would consume me, or something even more terrible was going to happen when I walked away. It reminded me of the fire-and-brimstone ministers who told me I was going to burn in hell. He never explained what I did wrong, but I was going to be punished for it anyway.

A flesh offering is, as I learned later, a tiny nick of flesh usually taken off of one's arm. A sharp blade is used to do this with and the resulting piece of flesh is placed inside a small piece of usually red cloth and tied into a bundle. It symbolizes the sincerity of one's prayer. It is usually used when one wants to give a tangible offering for a very specific prayer. I have since given many, many flesh offerings in my life. I guess I did it for the right reasons because lightening has not yet stricken me down.

MY FIRST SUNDANCE'S AND
LEADING AN ALL-WOMAN'S SWEAT LODGE

I began Sundancing back home in South Dakota. When I went back to Sundance the second year, they decided to start having Sundance in California. Dennis Banks, co-founder and one of the leaders of AIM, sought refuge in California because it was the only state that wouldn't extradite him back to South Dakota to be sentenced for the alleged rioting he'd started in Custer. William Janklow, who was the governor of South Dakota at the time, really had it out for the guys from AIM, because he saw them as troublemakers. In his view, Indians had never been civilized, and he and Dennis had had words regarding a young woman named Justina Running Deer. Justina babysat the governor's children and one night when he was taking her home, William Janklow raped young Justina. He got away with it. A couple of nights before they were to go to trial and Justina was supposed to testify against him, she was found dead. Dennis Banks helped shed a lot of light on that incident and tried to mobilize around it, so Janklow was not fond of Dennis at all. There was a fear that if Dennis went back to South Dakota, he probably wouldn't get justice and might wind up in the system, never to be seen again.

When Denis Banks came to California, the governor was Jerry Brown, a young man. He granted Dennis asylum in California, but it meant Dennis couldn't leave the borders of California. Dennis had pledged to Sundance and he was told that wherever he was, that he should dance, so he organized the Sundance at D-Q, the university the Native people had begun to organize. Those of us who lived in California shifted our commitment to support Dennis at the Sundance and that's how I wound up dancing in California. After I came back from that Sundance, I was working the evening shifts at the Indian Women's Lodge for alcohol treatment. They asked for an all-women's lodge. They said, we've been told that you can do this. They'd heard that when I first returned to the Los Angeles area that I had been learning to pour water for women's lodges. I had stopped off at Point Conception and been instructed by Archie Fire to run a lodge there

At Point Conception, we organized a thirteen-month occupation to stop a corporation from drilling on Chumash land. They wanted to build a liquid natural gas terminal off the coast of Point Conception, which are sacred grounds to the Chumash people. When I drove into the camp, a Lakota man named Robin Black Cloud and a man named Joe Bill, whose tribe I can't remember, met me, and they said, "The fire's all ready and the rocks are ready."

I said, "Oh, so we're having a sweat?"

They said, "Yeah."

We walked back in the woods to the sweat lodge and there was just the firekeeper and the three of us. I said, "Who's running the lodge?"

Robin Black Cloud said, "You."

I said, "Me?"

Bill said, "Yeah, Archie says that you've danced enough and you can do that now."

I said, "I've never run a lodge before."

They said, "Oh, you'll do okay."

When we went into the lodge, I tried to remember what I'd seen done. I'd never been taught formally.

During the last round, I heard a noise: a tiny squeak, squeak, squeak. I said, "What's that?"

Joe Bill said, "Shhhh, it's sister mouse, she's praying."

I thought, a mouse? In the lodge? I was squeamish. I had one hand resting on the ground and when I called for the door, all of a sudden something darted up my arm and across my shoulder, and tried to make it around my neck through my hair. I screamed and the mouse jumped off my shoulder and ran away. I thought those guys were going to pee their pants, they were laughing so hard inside that lodge.

That was the only time I'd run a lodge, but when they asked for this women's lodge, I thought, well I think I could do it. We had to go out to Topangaga Canyon. A man said, "I'll get the fire going and we'll see you at such and such a time." I would only do it on my day off because I didn't want to be accused of being paid to do it. At the time I was working evening shifts at the Women's Recovery Lodge. I signed out the van, loaded up the women, and we took off. Just as we got there, I could smell in the air that there was a fire that had water poured on it. I got out of the van, and as the women were getting out, I walked up to the fire keeper and he said, "Ernie Peters was here."

I said, "Oh, where's he at?"

He said, "Well, he left."

I said, "Oh. Well, why is the fire out?"

He said, "Ernie made me put it out. He said he didn't give you permission to run a lodge here."

I said, "Why?"

He said, "He just said that he didn't give you permission."

I thought, okay. I told the women and, of course, they were very disappointed.

Then about two days later, I was at work, and the director came in. He said, "Beverly, can you come here for a minute?" I made sure my post was covered and I followed him into the boardroom. All these people were sitting around the room in a big circle. In the middle of the circle, there was a chair. He said,

"Have a seat. I don't want you to think this is a kangaroo court." I sat down and he began berating me for going to Topanga Canyon and assuming I could run a lodge. Who did I think I was? He said I wasn't very respectful of men, and I didn't know my place. All the people in the room seemed to support him. They made all these veiled threats. My supervisor even said, "You know, this could cost you your job."

I guess I was supposed to be scared. But I wasn't. I was mad. Later, I told my cousin, my teacher Archie, about it and I said, "I don't understand. You told me I could do this."

He said, "I'll take care of it."

About two weeks later we went to an AIM meeting. Archie stood up and he said, "I want everyone here to know that next week I am taking Beverly Little Thunder up to Alta Dena. I have a place there and we're going to build a lodge for women and I'm teaching her. If there's anyone here who has any hassle or any gripe about this, you need to talk to me about it now. She is a relative, she is a Lakota woman, she has every right to do this, and no one has the right to tell her that she can't."

You could have heard a pin drop. I wanted to crawl under a table because I felt like I was sitting in the middle of that boardroom again. My early experiences with that level of patriarchy were part of what moved me to pledge to dance years prior. For sure, that's what took me to my first Sundance, and what led me to make my first pledge.

A pledge is when one commits to dancing for four days—without taking in any food or water for four days—for four years. It means serving the community and praying for those who are in need of prayers. It also means living your life as a positive example to others. It does not mean holding any special role in the community or title, as some believe.

MY SON RICK'S HORRIBLE, LIFE-ALTERING EXPERIENCES

In 1977, the government introduced eleven House bills, all aimed at decreasing or taking away the rights of Native people. Some of the bills were in direct conflict with Treaties that had been made with the Native peoples. As a result, on a national level, AIM was trying to draw attention to the bills so that mainstream people would be aware. Denis Banks and some of the big shots in AIM decided that they would organize a walk from San Francisco to Washington, D.C. They would leave in February from California and they would arrive in D.C. in July. The goal was to show up on the White House steps by the fourth of July. Their plan was to have tens and tens of thousands of people behind them. I wanted to go, but I couldn't with five kids. I just couldn't see dragging five kids on that kind of trip and I didn't have a vehicle that would have made it. But Rick wanted to go and some of the men said, well, let Rick go. I said, "He's only thirteen."

But the men in AIM said, "He's a young man and he needs this experience. We'll take care of him."

Several of the women pitched in and bought him a sleeping bag, some hiking boots, a jacket, and other things he needed, and he left to go on the march with these people. The last words that rang in my ears when I said goodbye to my baby were those of the men who said, "We'll take care of him."

Yet, while Rick was on the march, he was pretty much left to his own devices. From what I understand, he and the other kids ran wild. And a mother's worst nightmare, there was some sexual abuse going on. I don't know if it was between the older kids and the younger kids or if it was between adults and kids—I just know that my son said it happened, and that it happened to him. He talked about being woken in the mornings with a cattle prod.

I met him on the road in Colourado. I'd taken a train with Ernie Peter's wife. When we met up, everything that Rick had on was filthy. He had no clean clothes. His hair was very long and thick, and it was full of lice. I took him down to the showers and made him strip. I gave him a bar of soap and a bottle of shampoo. Then I went into town, washed all his clothes twice, went to the drug store to get some stuff to put in his hair, and went back. Poor thing. He had to sit there with a towel around him while I washed his hair again, and then deloused him with a fine-tooth comb. I asked him if he wanted to come home and he said, no.

These kids were taken along so they would have the numbers and so the media would see the kids marching, see that the kids were concerned about the future, too. Which was true, of course. They were very concerned. But they weren't cared for. They weren't honoured and cared for the way they should have been honoured and cared for as children.

When Rick came back, he was no longer a child; he was a young man. This happened around the time I was moving from Southern to Northern California.

I had met a man named Chemo Candalaria and his wife, Teresa. They had four children: two little girls and two little boys. Chemo was a Sundancer. He told me that he and his wife were moving to Northern California and buying fifty-five acres where they were going to create a community for Native families so that we could teach our children. Of course, I wanted that to happen, so I sold everything I owned. When I got up there, I gave him a huge amount of money and moved into a fifteen-by-fifteen cabin with a loft. There was only enough room for the four small children to sleep in the cabin. Chemo said, "Well, why don't you let Rick stay at our place," in the one house that was on the land. Unbeknownst to me, Chemo and his wife Teresa had pulled Rick into a sexual threesome.

Chemo and I locked horns continuously for the next three weeks. We argued about how the lodge area was cared for. I didn't like that he allowed dogs to sleep in the lodge and trash was tossed around it. We had differences about how the males were treated and the role of the girls and women on the land. His sons were abusive to the animals on the land and he just laughed and said that boys will be boys. The final straw came when a male guest tried to rape me. Chemo said he did not understand why it upset me. He told me I had given birth to five children so what did I have to lose? Finally Chemo left.

Two weeks later I found out that Teresa was pregnant. A week later I found out she was pregnant with Rick's baby and she told me she was going to have an abortion.

This was a horrible time for my son. When he learned that Teresa was pregnant, he came to me. I can't stress this enough: he was thirteen years old. Teresa was in her early thirties. That's when I found out that they had pulled him into a threesome. He, at thirteen, was not prepared to be a father, but he wanted to believe he was a man. He was crying and saying, "She's going to kill my baby." I called the police. They talked to her and they talked to him, and then proceeded to tell me that Rick was thirteen and he was just sowing his wild oats. They said there was nothing they could do about it, nor would they even consider doing anything about it. I went to the next Sundance meeting and talked about it, because Chemo was still a dancer there and Teresa had pledged to dance also. They said the same thing, that Rick was a young man, and he was sowing his wild oats and there was nothing they were going to do about it. I told the women and the women were enraged about it, but there was nothing they could do because the men wouldn't put their feet down and say Chemo couldn't dance The women confronted Teresa and told her they did not want to dance with her. So, Teresa wasn't allowed to dance as a woman, but the family was still permitted to be there. After that, Rick would not come to Sundance. And I was told that if I brought it up at Sundance, I would be escorted off the land.

Needless to say, it was a difficult time. There was very little support. I felt the message that was being sent to my son was twofold: that sexual abuse was okay and that there was nothing wrong with a young boy getting involved with an older woman. The message that this was sending to our young people enraged me. I said to Dennis Banks, "If this had happened to your thirteen-year-old daughter, what would you have done?"

He said, "Well, I would have killed the man who did that to her, but this is different. This is a boy."

I was left with either having to leave the Sundance community or not saying anything about it again. At that time, I was living in an unstable situation in Northern California. I was going to school and coping with everyday life at the same time. My children were everything to me. I was trying to survive, as a woman, a mother, an activist, a Sundancer.

THE TRIAL OF PAUL SKY HORSE AND RICHARD MOHAWK

I started getting involved with AIM, and its related activities, when I was about twenty-one. Ever since AIM's march on the Bureau of Indian Affairs in Washington, DC, in 1968, AIM was known as a "militant group." When I was at UCLA, there were riots that same year. A friend of ours was shot on the ear, right in front of us, and we had to go to court to testify. Then, during the Occupation of Alcatraz in 1969, I went out there and helped organize within the community. I made fry bread there—I've made more frybread in my life than anybody could make in two lifetimes. We organized concerts with Buffy Sainte-Marie, Floyd Westerman, and others. I attended rallies and protests throughout the years and I was involved in Vietnam's Mothers Against the War. It seemed like I was always marching and making a placard sign for something.

AIM was just forming in California about the time two young Native men, Paul Sky Horse, who was Mohawk, and Richard Mohawk, were arrested for the murder of a cab driver. From 1975 to 1977, the majority of my life, besides when I was with my kids, was taken up with Paul Skyhorse and Richard Mohawk, both of whom were a part of AIM. In Ventura Canyon, there was a hippie commune of sorts and somehow a bunch of Native people found their way there—mostly Native men. One of them had hooked up with a white woman who had invited him to the commune. The men talked their way into putting up a lodge, and then kind of moved in. One weekend, some of the people from the camp did some heavy partying in town at someone's house. That same weekend, the police found the body of an African American cab driver lying in a five-foot-diameter drain pipe, near the camp. What led them to the commune itself, I don't know, but just as the police arrived, they found a pile of things that were burned and the cab driver's effects were there—his wallet and stuff like that. They began an investigation and determined that it was someone at the camp who had murdered this man.

The cab driver's final fare was with people from the camp and he was last known to have two men and a woman in the car. I don't know what the circumstances were that led them to put out a warrant for Paul Skyhorse and Richard Mohawk. The first time I heard of it was in the newspaper, where the headlines read: "Body Found in AIM Camp No. 13." That was totally made up by the media. The camp was not an AIM camp. I guess when the police went to the camp to ask questions, a Native woman told them that it was Paul Skyhorse and Richard Mohawk who had done this. The police tracked the two men down in Arizona, in Phoenix I believe, arrested them and brought them back for questioning. They were then arrested and charged with murder. Of course, believing my brothers and sisters that these two men were innocent, and knowing how AIM and its members were constantly persecuted, I too believed in their innocence. I and others began working at the grassroots level to disseminate information and draw attention to the trial. The belief in AIM was that if we made the innocence of these two men public, there would be more eyes on the police and it would be harder for the authorities to cover things up. So we created the Paul Skyhorse Richard Mohawk Offensive Defense Committee

Our first few meetings were held in Los Angeles. I recall going to those meetings and having to bring my children with me because I had nowhere to leave them. They were looking for a co-chair for the committee. A man named Michael Mora, a Latino who was very active, had agreed to chair it, but he wanted a co-chair, and he wanted a woman. My sisters—while I was out of the room—immediately nominated me because I had told them I wouldn't mind doing that. So I was nominated and voted in before I knew it. Again, it was not without some resistance from the men. There was a man there named George Martin, who was from Alaska. I want to say he was Thinget, but I may be in error. He was very misogynist. I remember one day coming down the stairs—you had walk down these stairs to get to the door of the centre where we were meeting—with my youngest daughter Lushanya in my arms. I was walking behind him and inadvertently bumped into him. I apologized, then added, "We'll start rumours if I tumble down the stairs. People will be saying I fell for you."

He turned around at the bottom of the stairs and cussed me out. We weren't here to joke. This was serious. Two men's lives were on the line. The women with me were startled. I had apologized for almost coming down the stairs on top of him, so I was totally floored by his reaction to my bit of humour, and the women who heard him were upset with him for attacking me that way. But those were the kinds of things that were endured on a daily basis from different men. They were always rude. I said to him, "George, I need to thank you for teaching my young daughter that that's what she can expect from Native men. That that's how Native men will talk to her." He grumbled something and slammed into the building. He later came up to me and begrudgingly apologized. I said, "George, the damage is done. My daughter's already witnessed it." That was just the first of many run-ins I had with George Martin.

As the co-chair, I learned how to operate a mimeograph machine. I learned how to put together flyers and how to create wheat paste. I also learned how to speak in front of large groups of people. I have a picture of myself on stage in a park somewhere, holding Lushanya. We used to hold fry bread and chili feeds to raise money. We had all kinds of fundraisers really. We had concerts. A woman named Ruthy Gordon used to come and perform. So did Buffy Sainte-Marie, Floyd Westerman, and Jackson Browne. John Trudell, who was a big spokesperson for AIM at the time, would come and speak. Dennis Banks would come down, because Dennis was up in the Bay area, and together we would organize these events and draw some two or three hundred people.

We went to Ventura several times. Working with the legal team, we'd have demonstrations to raise public awareness. We got a change of venue from Santa Barbara in Ventura county, closer to home in L.A. county. Unfortunately, all the judges would not sit. They recused themselves because they'd all been at a dinner where a skit was performed that degraded Native people. They felt that having witnessed that skit, they couldn't be impartial, so they pulled a judge out of retirement—a very right wing judge. The case was held in a courtroom in L.A. that had a Plexiglas window between the gallery where the spectators sat and the area where the defendants and legal team sat, and only about thirty people were allowed into the courtroom at a time. Before entering, we were all searched. We couldn't to wear T-shirts that had any kind of logo on them and we couldn't wear sunglasses. It was a bizarre hearing. Every day at noon, when they took their break, we would go and sit in front of the federal building, where we would sing and drum, hand out flyers and leaflets, and watch as the FBI took pictures from across the street. In the upper part of the building, we could see their long cameras pointed at us, watching, taping.

As co-chair I was responsible for helping Michael Mora with the organizing. Michael lived in what they called the Offence Defense Committee House, an apartment in Los Angeles. I was still living in San Gabriel, so I had to drive an hour every day. As I said, I spent ninety per cent of my time there. I would go home, clean house, fix meals for my children, and get them off to school. A lot of the time I had would have to pack all of them in the car for the meetings in the evenings. At the end of the meeting, we'd drive home and I'd put the kids to bed, only to do more of the same the next day. The days I did get to spend at home, I was on making phone calls, organizing. It was a lot of work. I believed strongly in the innocence of these two men.

We had a many successes, and also a lot of setbacks. Meeting the bills, such as rent and utilities for the apartment we used to organize from, printing costs of the thousands of flyers and posters, and the small stipend required to cover the cost of food at the organizing house, was always a challenge, and we were constantly doing things to try to raise money. I remember donating half of my food stamps to the Offence Defense Committee so that they'd have money for food—sharing what I had, even though I had five children to raise. I made some lifelong friends during that time. My friend Marlene, who is Cherokee, is one of those friends, one of my teachers and mentors. There were others too, and these women were the ones who helped me with my children. Marlene was the one who introduced me to thrift stores. She would go to thrift stores to buy clothes for my children. One Christmas, she came over with an armload of presents, all gift-wrapped—a lot of them filled with things from thrift stores—nice things for the kids—because she knew that I didn't have the money to do that for them.

There was a group called Prairie Fire who worked for us and they were basically rich white kids who dressed like they were poor until they went home to visit their parents on holidays. They were there to help the Natives and their whole focus was on revolution and militancy. While they would do things—take pictures, help put together slide shows—we constantly had to remind them that the sacred pipe and militancy didn't go hand in hand. They created a poster that caused a big stink among our Elders because they manipulated a photograph to show a Native warrior with a pipe in one hand and a gun in the other. We tried to tell them that our power was in the pipe, our faith in the Creator, that the gun was not the way we were going to battle the government; we never had done it that way and we weren't going to start now. While they meant well and they tried to help, they also were part of our struggle.

It was through Prairie Fire that I first heard the word lesbian. For some reason I had to stay in town one night and I stayed in the apartment of a woman who had some books on lesbians. I remember devouring them and thinking, wow, this is what I am; this is who I am. Of course, in the Native community, that wasn't something you talked about. I didn't know any Native lesbians. The only lesbians I knew were white women. They were somewhat of a curiosity and not anything like me, so I knew I couldn't be lesbian because that's not the way I behaved or dressed or acted. I had talked to one of the women about how unhappy I was in my marriage and some of the stuff that had gone on and she said, "If you ever decide you want to leave your husband, you have sisters who would help you." I wasn't quite sure what that meant, so I just tucked it away in the back of my head.

The trial went on for two years. There were comical aspects. One time I went to court with Lushanya, who was still very little, and still in diapers. We didn't have paper diapers, or at least I didn't have paper diapers, so I used cloth diapers. I used to carry empty bread bags to put the diapers in. Lushanya had pooped her diaper and after I changed her, I had rolled it up, and tossed it into a bread bag, which I then closed tightly, figuring I would rinse it out when I got home because I didn't want to do that in a public bathroom. They always checked our bags before we entered the courtroom, so the guard had started fishing through the diaper bag. I tried to say something, but she told me to be quiet. She stuck her hand right into the diaper, and they didn't typically wear gloves in those days. After that, though, she started wearing gloves. Everybody laughed at that.

A woman named Julie Evening Lily came along and joined the Offense Defense Committee. Everyone suspected her of being an FBI agent. That was the big thing then because this happened shortly after Dennis Banks had discovered that one of the men in AIM, who had been his trusted confidant, was working with the FBI as an informant. If you said the wrong thing, you were immediately suspected of being FBI, and Julie was one of those people. A core message to many of us at that time was: don't rock the boat or say something contrary to anything that's going on because you'll be labelled as FBI.

One time, Dennis came down for a meeting that lasted all night. I fed my children and put them to bed. I asked the neighbour if she would check on them, and then I went to this meeting, which was only supposed to last a couple of hours. The sun was coming up the next morning and nothing had been resolved. They were still talking. I was tired and concerned about my children. I remember I snapped at Dennis, and said, "Dennis, some of us have children at home that we need to get back to."

He said, "I have children at home."

I said, "Yes, but some of us don't have women at home to take care of those children."

He said, "Well, if this isn't important to you, then go."

I felt like I was being challenged between what's more important: our children or these men's freedom. It was a very uncomfortable moment.

ARRESTED WITHOUT WARNING

During that time, I drove an old car. Thinking back, it cost only forty-four dollars to register it. We didn't have to have insurance at that time. But I didn't have the extra forty-four dollars. I got stopped three times and I was given warnings about not having a registration tag. We had an event where a group from Akwesasne called Quatro Flechas was travelling to L.A. They were primarily Elders and young people from South America who were travelling with some of the people from Akwesasne—Mohawks and Onondaga, who were raising cultural awareness. They called themselves The White Woods of Peace. We had organized places for them to perform where they could get small stipends for being there. One was a school. It wasn't too far from my home.

I had a friend who was a Salish Elder from Washington State. Adeline was disabled—she'd had polio as a child. In addition to going to pow-wows, sitting at tables, dancing, and being a part of the Indian Centre politics, I took her everywhere. I would take her shopping, to doctors' appointments, and to cultural events. At the pow-wows, we'd camp together. I'd take her out to the sweat lodge. So, she was in my old car often, and my children were usually stuffed in the back seat. All of a sudden I saw the lights come on and I thought, oh great, I'm being stopped again.

The officer got out of his car and walked up to me and said, "Beverly, can I have your license, please." I gave him my license and I didn't think about the fact that I hadn't given him my name. He said, "Where are you going?"

I said, "To an event. I'm taking this Elder and my children to a cultural event."

He said, "Well, you know you don't have tags for your car?"

I said, "I know."

He said, "I have a warrant for your arrest. Actually, I have three warrants."

I looked at him and said, "What am I supposed to do with my children?"

He said, "Well, why don't I follow you to the school and maybe someone there can take your kids."

It wasn't until I started driving that Adeline said, "How did he know where you were going? You didn't tell him where you were going." I realized then I'd been singled out. When we got to the school, there were people there who saw me drive up with the police car behind me and they came and asked what was going on. Everybody gathered around. I left my car, my children and Adeline there. The police arrested me and took me to the local jail.

When they drove me away from the school, they didn't put handcuffs on me. The officer said, "I won't put handcuffs on you in front of your children."

In the car, the officer said to me, "So, what are the Natives all upset about?"

I said, "It really isn't something I can talk about right now."

Then about a block before we got to the police station, they pulled over into an ally and he said, "Will you step out of the car?" I thought, oh great. I was scared. Roughly, he slammed me up against a wall and put these handcuffs on me, quite tight. When we got to the police station, he told the other officer, "Keep an eye on her. She's one of them AIMsters." I thought, how does he know that?

They put me in a cell and then they brought another woman. She kept trying to engage me in conversation but I wasn't talking. Finally, they let her out of the cell and two men in suits came. They stood outside the cell. One of them said, "We're going to be having a conversation here, young lady."

I'd been asking to make a phone call but they kept putting me off. Finally, one of the men in suits said, "Okay, you can make your phone call now."

I called the community house and I could hear all this activity in the background. Michael Moira, my co-chair of the offense/defense committee, said, "Your bail is set at three thousand dollars. If we come up with three hundred and twenty we can get you out. We're just taking up a collection and someone's on their way over there to bail you out."

I said, "They're talking about transferring me over to Sible Brand."

He said, "Well, we can't let that happen."

I hung up and one of the men said, "Where's your buddies at now?" I just looked at him and he said, "Oh, the silent treatment. That's okay. We have ways of making people talk." And I thought, oh, great. When you're in a cell, time feels like forever.

Someone finally came to the cell and said, "Oh, you're lucky." Michael was there and he had bailed me out. They had put together the money to pay my fines for not having tags for my car. I remember being frightened, really frightened. Because up until that point I'd never been arrested, even around organizing. I knew that horrible things happened to organizers who'd been arrested and this was after Anna Mae had been killed.

When I got out, George Martin and some of the other men were asking how I got out so fast. What was that all about? Oh, she's probably an informant. That's what they thought. Then I had that to battle with. Fortunately, Michael Moira knew that wasn't the case. There were many people who knew that wasn't the case. But, it was hard. I felt like I was walking on egg shells after that. But it was worth it for me because I believed that the work I was doing would ensure freedom for my children. That it was going to further the struggle we as Native people in this country were facing and that my children wouldn't have to deal with these same injustices. I believed that our work would set a precedent so that future generations could look back and say, look, this was a pattern. It never once occurred to me that what I was doing was for nothing or that it wasn't making a difference at all.

REGALIA IN THE COURTHOUSE

During the trial of Paul Sky Horse and Richard Mohawk, a well-known medicine man, Leonard Crow Dog, came to town to testify. Leonard Crow Dog showed up at court in regalia. The judge saw him and said, "You're not coming into my courtroom half dressed. You will wear a tie in my courtroom." He recessed the morning and said, "We will resume at one o'clock and you will be in a tie or the entire team will be held in contempt of court." So we all left.

Several of us went to a local Salvation Army and we bought the most outrageous tie we could find. At one o'clock Leonard was back in the courthouse in regalia, with a tie. When the judge walked in, he was sitting at the table with the defense committee and the judge went into a rage. Our lawyer stood up and said, "But, Your Honour, your instructions were that he be back here at one o'clock with a tie. He is sitting in this courtroom. He was here at one o'clock, and he is wearing a tie. Perhaps we misunderstood what your instructions were. I would ask that the transcriber read back your last words." So, she was ordered to read them and all he had said was to be back at one o'clock with a tie. The lawyer said, "You said nothing about not being in regalia. You said nothing about a shirt or a suit. You said, wearing a tie. This is dragging on to ridiculous. I would like these proceedings to continue in the interest of time. This is a long, drawn out trial and I think this is just a further distraction." So the judge allowed his testimony to go on, with Leonard Crow Dog in regalia. Of course, we all sat back and we couldn't laugh out loud, but we laughed about it a lot afterward.

THE STARFISH AND THE GIRL

It was towards the end of the trial of Paul Sky Horse and Richard Mohawk that I heard a story about a man walking on a beach with a little girl. The little girl was busy picking up starfish and throwing them back in the ocean. The old man asked, "What are you doing?" She said, "Well, I'm giving them a chance at life." He said, "Well, there must be thousands and thousands and thousands of starfish. There's no way you can possibly make a difference." She looked at him, picked up a starfish and threw it as far into the ocean as she could. She said, "I made a difference in that one's life."

I believed that everything I did made a difference in someone's life, that each day that I got up I made a difference in at least one person's life, as others made a difference in mine each day. I was zealous about what I was doing. I did it wholeheartedly. I began learning about our political history as a Native people and for a while I leaned very heavily on the Native perspective, never bothering to look at the other side, only seeing our position. And that's how my children grew up. Some people would have said I was angry—and I was. I told them I had a right to be angry. But what I was, really, was passionate. And, in retrospect, I realize that passion was part of a process of coming back to my centre and beginning to learn and develop the skills to look at a situation from all angles, understanding that I didn't have to take sides. It was not necessary for me to say, this is right or this is wrong. I had no right to do that. It was not in my life contract. But at that time I believed it was, and I think that a lot of us were taught that we have the right to make those judgments.

Paul and Richard were acquitted. We were so excited. It was cause for celebration. We very quickly planned a celebratory event the day after they got out of jail. We all went to jail to witness their release. Of course, the media and everybody was there. During the entire process, we'd been talking about bringing to light the issues that were prevalent among Native people across the country—the poverty, the lack of jobs, the alcoholism, the growing drug problem, our youth and their suicides, the forced sterilization of our women, the murder and disappearance of our women. All of these issues were coming to light and they were issues that we also included in our educational sessions. The land issues, too, were important. At that time the Navaho and the Hopi were engaged in a battle over Big Mountain and Peabody mine. We helped to fuel that fire, to raise awareness about that issue and others. Like the fishing right struggles. There were so many struggles.

Even today, if you sat down and made a list of all of the struggles that Tribes are embroiled with—with the government, with governmental agencies—you'd probably have ten full pages, and that would just be a list of what those issues were. During that time, I also learned about the difference between socialism and communism and all the different social structures that had been attempted throughout the world. I learned about Cuba and about what was going on there. I even made a clandestine trip to Cuba by way of Mexico through an organization that was sneaking people into Cuba and allowing them to see firsthand what was going on there with the Cuban people. Of course, I realize now that we were shown what they wanted us to see, but at that time, I believed. I trusted in everything. I know now that everything is not always as it seems, that you can slant anything to be what you want it to be. You can just throw the things you don't want people to see under the rug. Nothing is black and white. There are many shades of grey in between.

DRUGS AND ALCOHOL AND THE CEREMONIAL COMMUNITY

When Leonard Crow Dog was brought to town for the trial, I got to know his wife Mary, who was a very young Lakota woman. She had written two books, *Lakota Woman* and, *Okitika Woman*. In the first book, she mainly talked about Leonard Crow Dog, her wonderful husband, and in the next one she blasts him. That aside, the couple were put up in a motel. Mary was there with her little boy. I prepared dinner at my home and went all out—made enchiladas and rice and beans and fry bread and a big cake. Everyone came out to greet Leonard Crow Dog, and shared this meal, but Mary and her son Pedro were not with them. I asked, "Where is your wife and your son?"

Leonard said, "She's back at the motel."

I said, "Well, you have to take some food back to her." I put together some food to take to her as well as some snack stuff for the baby.

Afterward, he said, "We're going to have a Native American Church ceremony tonight and I want you to be there." Okay, but I had to run around to find someone to take care of my children. Another woman and I—she too had to find someone to care for her children—later piled into my car and we headed up to Santa Barbara. We got there around ten o'clock. They were already out at the teepee.

They said, "Come in, we're waiting for you."

I didn't know anything about peyote. That's what they gave us during the ceremony. I got very, very sick, which they told me might happen. The doorman walked me back to the teepee and said, "This is a good thing. The medicine is working."

The next morning when I left the teepee, I remember stepping outside and thinking, this is a really powerful medicine, but this is not my way. I knew at that moment I'd never go to another Native American Church ceremony.

After the ceremony, I started to see things differently, I started to scrutinize some of the leadership and I began to realize that a lot of them used alcohol and drugs. John Trudell, one of the most eloquent speakers of modern times for Native People smoked marijuana, and that's just one example of so many.

In my mind, I couldn't put following a spiritual path and using a substance to get high together in a good way. They just would not come together. I couldn't see how utilizing those things in the way they were being utilized could have any good coming from them. What I saw instead was people who were unmotivated, focusing on where their next high or drink would come from, ignoring their families, abusing their children, and abusing their wives. Then they'd show up at sweat lodge and talk about how you shouldn't come to the lodge under the influence, and that drugs and alcohol were weapons used to destroy our people.

I began to become acutely aware of how I wanted to live my life. Some people would say I was prudish or judgmental, but I did not want to live my life that way any more. It didn't make sense to me. I didn't want to hear a child saying, oh, yeah, I went to sweat lodge with Beverly and learned how to pray, learned how to connect with Mother Earth, and two days later I saw her falling down drunk. That, for me, was a contradiction.

All this time, as these ideas and thoughts were developing, Paul Sky Horse and Richard Mohawk were released from jail. The next day, we had a celebratory gathering for them, and they showed up drunk. They came late and they stayed a very short time. Had they shown up on time they would have had the media at their beck and call, because every station in town was there. We didn't even have make a call or write a press release, which was new. They had the opportunity to make a statement on behalf of Native people that would have been heard, and they passed that up because they arrived late and drunk. It was a slap in the face. For two years many of us had been supporting them. I learned a lot about what my expectations were and it wasn't necessarily what their expectations were for themselves. They just wanted to get out of jail so they could resume living their lives the way they'd lived them before they'd been incarcerated. I felt like we had just been a means to an end, all of us who'd worked so hard for them to be freed.

I was crushed when, two years later, both of them tried to rob a bank, wound up shooting a single mom, and were arrested. I was crushed when for a short period of time, Kenny, and my children and I, stayed at the home of Richard Mohawk and his wife, Lisa, and their child. I saw that every morning when he got up, Richard had to have a joint. Every hour on the hour he was smoking a joint. He said to me, "You know, that cab driver had it coming. He asked for it." This revealed to me that there was a good possibility Paul Sky Horse and Richard Mohawk had indeed killed that cab driver. I felt like two years of my life had been taken from me and my children because I believed these men were innocent. I learned a lot about organizing during that time. That was a blessing. But it was also a disaster.

A HIT ON MY LIFE

After the trial ended, the Longest Walk Started, so for a time our whole focus was around the Longest Walk. There was no need for the women any more, so George Martin, Ernie Peters and other men within the AIM ranks, kind of pushed us aside. But we continued doing the work we'd been doing: going to pow-wows, distributing information, handing out flyers, organizing. Dennis Banks came to see the Los Angeles chapter of AIM and said he wanted to organize a big pow-wow to honour the walkers reaching D.C. His idea was to have big a pow-wow and a rock concert in every large town, and invite all the Native people to attend. Everybody on the committee was rushing around saying, Dennis said we have to do this, Dennis said we have to do that. He wanted to hold the event in Los Angeles, at the coliseum, which holds thirty-five thousand people. To secure the coliseum, we needed twenty-five thousand dollars and we didn't have twenty-five thousand dollars. Nor did we have any way to raise it. We didn't even have anyone who would agree to perform. What we had was Native people going to the homes of stars and trying to jump the fences to convince them they needed to do this.

Six weeks before the event in D.C. was supposed to happen, Dennis came down and asked, "What have you guys done?"

The man who was spearheading said, "Well, we couldn't do this and we couldn't do that."

Myself and a Native woman named Lois Red Elk stood up and said, "You know, we've been taught that when you honour somebody, when you are proud that someone has accomplished something, you have a giveaway. Why couldn't we just have a big feed and pow-wow at a park? Get a drum to donate their time, get a park permit? It might cost us a hundred dollars. Get people to donate. Let's just have a big feed."

And someone yelled, "Yeah, and who's going to organize that?"

Lois and I said, we will. So between the two of us, we managed to get hamburgers and hot dogs and chicken donated. One restaurant donated gallons and gallons of potato salad. We got a drum and we had a big pow-wow to honour the people from the Longest Walk. It went off quite well.

But the men were really mad. They were angry at Lois and I, and said that we had overstepped our bounds. That's not what Dennis wanted. We said, regardless of what Dennis wanted or not, you guys weren't able to pull it off and we wanted to do something. Then Lois's house was broken into. She had a button collection that was stolen. Other things were stolen from her house too. And her car tires were flattened. A lot of other strange things started happening. A woman's car caught fire outside a laundromat after she was challenged by a woman who was in really tight with the men. A certain Native woman was accused of doing that. We went to a meeting where she was confronted and put on the hot seat. She was furious because the man who told her to set fire to that woman's car did not stand up and back her. When we came out of the meeting, she was really upset. When Lois and I tried to console her, she said, "Well, you know, he wanted me to shoot you, Beverly."

I said, "What?"

We went to a restaurant, we sat down, and she proceeded to tell us her story. When she began to talk, some things that had happened began to fall into place in bits and pieces. Earlier, she'd invited me to a pow-wow they were having out at her reservation in California, out in the desert. I was going to go, but that morning Lushanya was sick and I couldn't travel with her. So, I didn't go and I had no way of getting in touch with the woman. When I saw her again, we were at an event at the Exposition Centre. I told her, "Yeah, I wasn't able to make it."

She just smiled and said, "It's okay. It wasn't meant to be."

At that same event at the Exposition Centre, this man came up to me and said he was really hungry but he didn't have any money, so we bought him some food and a cup of coffee. As we were standing there, while he was eating, the same woman walked over to us. She looked at him and she said, "What if I had done what you wanted me to do? You wouldn't be standing there stuffing your face, would you?" He just looked at her and said,

"Oh, leave me alone." She looked back at him with disgust and walked away. She was quite angry.

In the restaurant, the woman proceeded to tell us that this man had instructed her to invite me to the pow-wow out at her reservation, to take me up into the desert, shoot me and just leave me there. She didn't know that I had children. In fact, she didn't know anything about me. She said, "That's what AIM has always had me do. I didn't know that you had children. I didn't know about the work that you and Lois do. I was just told that you were being a nuisance."

I looked at her and I said, "You would have gone ahead and done that?"

She said, "Yeah. But, I wouldn't now because I know you, but at that time you were just someone who was being a nuisance. When I came to the Exposition, remember what I said to that guy? That's what I meant. What if I had done what he'd asked? You wouldn't have been buying him food."

The way she had said it, Lois and I both knew she was dead serious. That was when I decided I needed to leave Southern California.

DENANAWIDAH-QUETZALCOATL UNIVERSITY

When I left L.A. I didn't leave the AIM movement. I got involved with the politics through D-Q University. D-Q stands for Deganawidah-Quetzalcoatl, a place where Native American peoples could learn in their own ways. The first part of the name is meant to be used only in a spiritual context, so the university became known as D-Q. And, of course, then it was the time of International Treaty Council, so we were doing a lot of work to get the treaties ratified. The California tribes also had their struggles, and we were involved with that. It was a crazy time. As I look back now, I don't know how I made it through those years. There was always something going on. There were many people who were supportive and there were women in my life who helped and supported me, but there were definitely challenges. But the man I was married to during this time, Kenny, and his constant binging stretched my finances. The happiest years I had with him were the ones when he was gone most of the time. I kept hoping he'd never come back, but like a bad penny, every three months or so, he'd call and come back.

During this time, Governor Jerry Brown had been voted out after ten years in office, so at the end of that year, On the AIM front, we had to get Dennis Banks out of California, otherwise he would have been extradited. So we were heavily involved in that as well. Also, we had Sundance meetings every month. I had to drive seventy-five miles to get to the Sundance, spend the weekend there, and then drive seventy-five miles back. It was very difficult financially. I raised my children during those years on five hundred and seventy-five dollars a month. That was my total income for the month, plus any extra money I could generate from selling my beadwork. That's a skill that I'm really glad I've always had. Still, I don't know how I did it. Two hundred and seventy-five dollars went for rent. Sometimes I think, oh, things were cheaper then. But even so, the cost of gas alone to go back and forth ate up so much of our monthly income. Even though gas was cheaper then, still, it was a big chunk. I must have been crazy. That's all I can think about it now. I must have been crazy.

INFORMANTS INFILTRATE AIM

Around that time, there was a man named Frank Montellongo, an Apache, who started coming to the meetings. He drove an old Ford truck. He was a construction worker, always dressed in dirty jeans and a T-shirt. Balding. But he was always there. He brought wood for the lodge. He'd always show up with something new done. He was always there, standing in the background, willing to do whatever needed to be done. Just before I left Southern California, Frank called me and told me that the politics of what was going on was getting to be too much for him, and that he was leaving and going back to Phoenix because there was more construction work in Phoenix. He wanted to let me know that he really appreciated me, my family and my kids, and wished us well. I asked him to keep in touch and he said he would try. A year later, when I had moved to Northern California, I got a phone call from a man with the *LA Times*, who asked, "What do you think about Frank Montellongo being an informant for the police department?"

I said, "Well, they're always starting up rumours about someone."

He said, "This isn't a rumour. I have his police employment record in front of me."

I said, "Can you give me your number? Can I call you back?"

He said, "Yes."

So I hung up and I called Michael Moira, who lived in Ventura County, and I told him about the phone call. He said, "Beverly, it's true. It's true. He was seen in uniform, so an investigation has been conducted, and yes, he is a policeman."

A lot of organizations—mostly organizations of people of colour, of course—had been infiltrated by policemen in the LAPD. One woman had even married one of the undercover agents and had two children by him, and he'd continued writing about her. I went to the American Civil Liberties Union office and they had two thousand, two hundred and fifty-five pages of reports Frank Montellongo had written about me. He had even recorded some of my prayers in the sweat lodge. This man had taken my mother and I to pow-wow, he'd come to my home, and he'd had meals with me and my family. I felt so betrayed. I wound up getting several thousand dollars from a class action lawsuit, but it was years before I wanted to get involved in anything again, because I didn't trust anybody.

6.

COMING OUT

WHEN WE LIVED IN Northern California, people would come because we were between Reno and Sacramento and San Francisco, and our house was the stopping point. I often had whole families show up in the middle of the night and I'd have to have food for them the next day. I used to get fish from the fish hatchery—big salmon. I would wrap them and put them in the freezer. We'd have deer meat and I would gather berries and wild apples, so I always had a lot of food in my freezer. I would make blueberry pancakes and everyone thought, oh, Beverly makes blueberry pancakes or wild roast venison, baked salmon. They thought I was going way out for them and what they didn't know was, that's all I had. I served what I had. People would say, oh she always fixes these gourmet meals and I had to laugh. I still do the same thing today. That's why there's so much food on my shelves, because people are always coming. There's always going to be someone else at the table.

That's how I knew that my partner, Pam Alexander, was the right person for me. Our dinners were part of the process of getting to know her. Pam relocated from Maryland to Minneapolis in April 1998. A few months later, my son Gary sent his daughter Aris to spend the summer with me. Her mother had left and my son was unable to work and afford childcare for the summer. Aris moved in with me and Pam after that. One evening Pam came home from work with several very expensive steaks, wrapped in bacon. She said, "Who's going to be here tonight for dinner?"

I said, "Just me and you and Aris."

Beverly and Pam, 2006..

She said, "Okay" and put out three of these steaks.

Then the phone rang. It was two of my friends and I said, "Well, why don't you come on over and have dinner with us." So, she put out two more steaks. By the end of the evening, there were twelve people around the table. It was a feast. Pam fixed dinner that night and never blinked an eye. She never expressed any kind of irritation. She just kept saying, "Okay."

I said to her, "You know, if this had happened with my ex-lover, Caryl, she would have had a fit, because these people hadn't made reservations in advance." Then I said, "Thank you. This is my life."

She said, "It's okay. That's what we've got a freezer for." I knew then that she was the right person. And she's still like this. She really is amazing.

The time in Northern California was also a time that I was learning. Archie Fire was still at D-Q and he would take me aside and teach me. One of the sisters sat down and taught me the songs. We spent hours in a room, just sitting and singing over and over again, to learn one song. A lot of things happened during that time. And, it was part of my learning. One of the Elders in

California taught me the moon song for the women's full moon ceremony. So, on top of all the struggle, there was also a lot of singing and learning.

There was a group in Chico about twenty-five miles away, called the Feminist Women's Health Centre. It was the group responsible for *Our Bodies Ourselves*, a national group concerned with women's health and sexuality. It was a place that women could go to for an abortion. I started volunteering there and, of course, being in nursing and being in school, it was a good place to get some hands-on experience. Up until that time, I had only had my own earlier experience with wanting to abort a fetus. The result of having not done that for me had been a positive experience. I hadn't completely understood why someone would want to have an abortion, but working there I began to understand, to gain a full perspective instead of having an opinion about, "this is right or this is wrong." I realized, again, there was no black or white. Every woman deserved the opportunity, if she chose to, to have a safe and clean environment to have an abortion where she did not have to fear dying as a result. The group of women who staffed the clinic were largely lesbians. I began to see women in relationships with one another, something totally new to me.

This was during the time that I lived on Chemo and Teresa's land, the fifty-five acres that had once been a commune. People began to refer to it as Rattlesnake Gulch because there were lots of rattlesnakes there. There was a wooden shed that was filled with junk—books, magazines, clothes, cooking utensils, broken furniture. Chemo was systematically burning everything in the shed. He said, "This is all the junk that the women who used to live here left. We had to clean out the house so that we could move in." He asked me to help one day, so I was burning stuff and one of the things I picked up was some mimeographed sheets of papers that were stapled together, called *Lesbian Connection*. At that time the newspaper was very new. It came out in 1973 and was put out by a group of lesbians in Lansing, Michigan— letters, articles. I tucked it under my shirt and when I went back to my cabin, I stuck it under the mattress. When Kenny, my fourth husband, was in town, I would pull it out and read it. I thought, there are other people out there who are lesbians. That's what I am. I am a lesbian. I cried because I had a word for who I was. I couldn't burn any of those books any more because I realized it had been a group of lesbians who had lived there. And I have since actually met some of the women who lived there at that time, and the story they tell of how Chemo ran them off is very different from the story he told me.

That was my first exposure to lesbian literature, so going over to the Feminist Health Centre and working with these women, I realized that there was a whole subculture that I had no awareness of. I began to long for that kind of a relationship because it seemed so much gentler than what I had experienced. It felt safe and it felt right. Kenny knew that I was a lesbian and he said, "If you try to leave me, I'll tell everybody that you're a lesbian." That terrified me. I knew that since I was a pipe carrier and as a Sundancer, that coming out as a lesbian would not be greeted with respect. So, I kept quiet about it. But I started going over to Chico and working at the health centre and I told my husband I had a job there. Because I was in school, I would go over there a lot. I was enthralled with these women, but afraid to say that I was like them. When I finally told someone that I thought I was lesbian, and told them about the relationship I had with Mary Ann when my husband and I had split up, and how that ended because he threatened to take me to court, the woman wanted to set me up with someone.

And set me up she did. Right around this time, a woman doctor came into town. I'll never forget it because it was the day Prince Charles and Diana got married and it was all over the TV. This doctor and I went out. She was staying in a hotel and I had to go to school the next morning. But she suggested I spend the night with her at the hotel instead of driving back home. I said, "Okay." When we got to the room, she had a shower, I had a shower, and then we lay next to each other on the bed and went to sleep, watching the coverage of Diana and Charles' wedding. I didn't have the nerve to make a move and she didn't have the nerve to make a move. Dido, the woman who had set us up, was furious. She said, "She's been out a long time. She knows you're just coming out." When I think about it now, I think it's funny, but back then I thought, oh, I'm not attractive to her.

During that time, living on that mountain, I realized that I needed to make some serious changes. When I was dancing at D-Q, we were so close to San Francisco that we had a lot of gay men and women who came. When the men came and pledged to dance, I would hear some of the so-called leaders making hurtful, homophobic remarks—there was always a core group who did that, usually people who had danced a long time. It was primarily men, though. But there were also women. Besides me, there were three other women at this camp, Pearl, Carol and Ellen, who formed the core of the women there, which is why we had to go to all those meetings.

At a Sundance meeting, when they would bring up the subject of Bill dancing (I'm just making up that name), someone would say, yeah, well, he's kind of funny; he's limp-wristed. Well, is he going to dance as a woman or a man? Is he making a dress or a skirt? Do you want him sleeping in the teepee with you? Yeah, on the other side of the teepee. They would say terrible things. I would just cringe. I remember one time they had a big meeting and a group of women came up from San Francisco. One of them was an Elder. She's now passed. She had some health problems. She came with her cane and she and her group sat at a table where they had all this literature on gay resources and AIDS. A group of Native men from D-Q went out, shoved all of the literature in a trash can and physically escorted—dragged—these women off the land. They said, "Your kind isn't wanted here. Get out of here." I watched and I didn't say anything. I couldn't.

Then one woman came to dance who had been for some time with this man who was also a dancer. She was an artist. He had taken a knife and slashed all of her paintings, all of her canvases, and all of her clothing. She had three children. She was terrified to come to dance that year because he was going to be there. So I said, I'll run interference. She came and danced that one year, but she never came back. I knew she was a lesbian. I met her former male partner, but I didn't have the courage to stand up for her. There were others like that. Each year I felt more and more guilty because I sat there and said nothing. I realize now that it was internalized homophobia. I was afraid someone would know who I was.

I remember that I went to D-Q—the school the Chicano and Local Native people developed on an old air force communication base—in the middle of the week to pick something up, some papers and stuff that I had been working on, and Dennis Banks was there. He came out to the car with me. I was with my lover Melissa. We were on our way to San Francisco. She was very butch-looking. He said, "Who's that?"

I said, "My friend. She's driving with me to San Francisco. We're going to go to the Treaty House to do some work there."

He said, "She looks like a dyke."

I said, "She's gay."

He said, "Well what are you doing with her?"

I said, "Dennis, I just told you she's driving me. She's a nice person."

He said, "Well, you be careful."

I thought, it's a little late for that. I was really upset. I just wanted to get out of there as quick as I could.

Beverly Little Thunder (in the middle), with friends, at San Francisco Pride Day, 2003.

CAMP YELLOW THUNDER

We did a lot of organizing at D-Q and one year there was a camp that settled in the Black Hills called Yellow Thunder. They were fighting for the treaty rights of the Black Hills. All these women and children had moved up there. They were living in tents but winter was coming up and it was quite cold, so they put up a yurt. I went up there with the Feminist Women's Health Centre. That was during the time when the centre was promoting self-examinations, and they were teaching women how to use a mirror and a speculum to look at their own cervix. We'd all sit in circles and look at ourselves and at each other. They were trying to teach this self-exam to women. So I said, "Well, I'll go. I'm a Native woman and it'll make it easier." We set up a tent and, oh my god, you'd of thought we were going in there and having sex. The men and some of the women at the camp were not happy. The men sent the women over to tell us that Native women didn't need that. I said, "Yes, Native women do need this. We need to know our own bodies. We need to take control of our own bodies." They said we were promoting abortion and the genocide of our children. I tried to run interference, but we didn't get to keep the tent. We had to leave.

I knew some of the women, so when they set up the Yellow Thunder camp, I was in touch with these women. "What do you all need up there? Denis is getting ready to have a big fundraiser. I'm going to have a fundraiser simultaneously, but I want to know what it is you need," I asked them. So many times I'd seen money donated to camps that didn't get used for the people, as it had been intended. Instead, it got used for the leader. I'd seen Denis Banks get out of limos, I'd seen him go back to his teepee and have steaks for dinner while everyone else was eating thinned-down soup and fry bread. I'd seen that with my own eyes. So I said, "I want to know what you need. What do the women and the children need?"

They said they needed a cook stove and a chain saw, because it was hard to chop the wood, so I organized a fundraising event to raise the money for those things. I only had the help of the Feminist Women's Health Centre. We organized a deer and salmon feed. The salmon was donated and someone went out and got a deer for us. We roasted the venison and baked the salmon. We made cornmeal pudding. It was really good. We made fry bread and stewed blackberry pudding. We marketed the feast as a traditional Native meal, accompanied by a film and speakers who would give a talk about Yellow Thunder Camp. We made seventeen hundred dollars, and Native people were allowed to attend for free. The event was a big success.

We bought two chain saws and a wood stove and paid someone to bring them to the camp. We were also able to give the women four hundred dollars buy food with. Denis was really angry because he wasn't a part of it. He didn't come and speak. I didn't give the money to him. I accounted for the money, every penny of it, and sent it on my own. I said to him, "I didn't want to see it eaten up in media expenses. I wanted the money to go to the people. You take care of the media part of it. I'll take care of the things that are needed. That's what women do." Oh, he was mad.

There were several lesbians who had volunteered to help and they were pretty funny. We had all this venison. I'd put it into aluminum pans, seasoned it, then covered it with foil. I lived twenty-five miles away, so I couldn't cook the venison at my house. We were able to cook the salmon at the church where we held the event, but we couldn't cook the venison there because it needed to be in the oven a lot longer. So, I said, "I need seven ovens here in town where I can drop the venison off. All you have to do cook it in your oven, and at four o'clock I will come around and gather them all up."

The women said, "I'm a vegetarian. I've never had any meat in my oven," and, "Oh, I couldn't cook Bambi," or "I don't know if I could do that."

I said, "Ladies, I'm not asking you to eat the deer, I'm asking you to cook it. You don't even have to touch the foil."

Finally, I found the seven ovens I needed to roast the venison. Later, half of the women who had offered the ovens were sitting at the table eating the venison and saying, "Oh, this is so good!" That made me laugh out loud. It was always lesbians who helped with organizing and with the events. It wasn't straight women.

I think my coming-out process started there, during the organizing of the Yellow Thunder Camp event. I started spending more and more time in that community. They all knew that I was still married to Kenny. My lover, Melissa, was also aware that I was married. She and I were together for almost two years. We eventually broke up because she was moving and I didn't want to move. She was talking about needing to live in the city because she was a journalist and I didn't want to move into the city. So, we broke up. But we're still friends today. I still love her dearly, but I just didn't want to live in the city. She still lives in the city. During that time my husband would take off on drinking binges. He'd be gone for three months at a time, which made it easy to continue with my love life and still be married. Yellow Thunder Camp was really the catalyst for my coming out.

7.

MY SUNDANCE PLEDGE

M Y EARLY EXPERIENCES with the level of patriarchy among the Native men—and among some of the women—was part of what moved me to pledge to Sundance. For sure, that's what took me to my first Sundance. My husband at the time, Caesar, was not enthusiastic about me going to Sundance and felt that I should stay home and take care of my children. I felt strongly however that I needed to be at Sundance. I was drawn there.

I was told, as a woman, that it was my responsibility to teach my children, but how could I teach my children what I myself didn't know? If someone didn't also teach me, how could I teach them? And if that was my responsibility, it was my responsibility to find someone to teach me so that I could then pass on those teachings to my children.

So, I went to Sundance.

My first Sundance was in Green Grass, South Dakota, in 1977. I spent my time in the kitchen cooking. I jumped in where I thought I could start, and, actually, being in the kitchen cooking and supporting the others who were dancing was what I thought my role at Sundance should be. At that time, it had not occurred to me that I could also dance. I didn't have many opportunities to go out to the ceremonial arbor or space dedicated for dancing. Those who were dancing and fasting danced in the centre of the circular area, while supporters and singers sat under the shade of the branches used to create the arbor. During the Sundance itself, I spent most of my time in the kitchen! But the second time I went to Sundance, though I pretty much helped with the same things I did at the first Sundance, on the last day I was given an opportunity to go to the arbor.

It wasn't until I saw one of my sister's sons, who was fifteen at that time, dancing in that arbor, that I had my own vision. My nephew was very fair. If you were to see him, you would think he was white. He had sandy blond hair and hazel eyes. His mother had diabetes and her leg had been amputated. She was so young still. The men convinced him that he should dance for his mother, so he did. And he got sunburned. He turned brilliant red from the sun, sunburned beyond belief, and when they pierced through his sunburned skin, he screamed. The piercing was done by the men as a way of showing the sincerity of their prayers. Much like a baby is attached to the mother by an umbilical cord, the men dancing are connected to the sacred tree by a rope. I was told that the pain from this act was similar to the pain of birth experienced by women as they birthed their children. His entire body was a bright scarlet red. You could see it was difficult for him to even walk. They took him out there—it was the last day. His screams echoed in my heart. Can you imagine being sunburned and having someone touch you and then cut into your flesh? As he danced with the pegs buried into his chest, he didn't even get enough strength to pull back and break the thongs that were holding the pegs.

Men were required to dance until the rope was taut enough to break the pegs they were attached to. Sometimes when a man did not break quickly, other men would take him by the arms and dance him backwards until the pressure causes the skin to rip. I could see how frightened my young nephew was and how much pain he felt when the rope tugged at him. He would freeze up and he wouldn't dance. Two big men walked up to him and led him to the tree. They were encouraging him, trying to get him to jerk slightly and break, break that skin. Ultimately, they grabbed him under the arms and ran him backwards. His skin ripped. You could hear the snap of the flesh and he screamed. I was watching and I thought, oh my god. Then they ran him around the circle and everybody hooped and hollered and I thought, this is a circus. I knew there must be some underlying meaning to it, so I watched very carefully, hoping to understand.

Each time the dancers went around the tree at Sundance, they would bring out four or five pipes. Since there were so many men dancing, they needed quite a few pipes, so it wasn't uncommon for five or six people to present pipes at one time. I found myself face-to-face with a young man, a dancer, who presented me with his family's pipe. No one had admonished me at that time not to look at the dancers, so I looked him straight in the eye and all I saw was agony, pure agony. Tears were pouring down his face. I thought, if this young man can do this for his mother, I can do this for my children and for the people. So, when the dancers made their pledges, I stepped forward. I wasn't quite sure what I was doing when I pledged, but I stepped forward. I don't even know if my nephew ever realized the impact he had on me that day, and then over the years. I saw him again on other occasions. He had gotten married and he'd had children. His mom had died, and he hadn't finished the four years he had pledged to the Sundance. He backed away from the ceremony completely. That taught me that it was important for our children to have a good experience. You can't take a child out there and expect them to participate in ceremony and know what they're doing when they are too young. And even if they think they know what they're doing, you need to give them time to mature enough to fully understand the commitment they're making. They need the teachings.

RICK AND LUSHANYA SUNDANCE

My oldest son, Rick, Sundanced when he came back from the Longest Walk, held in 1978, to bring attention to Native Sacred Sites. Rick was born premature, and with only one kidney. The other kidney didn't develop, so when he fasted for Sundance, he had a really hard time. Then the first day he danced, they wound up having to take him to the emergency room because he collapsed from dehydration. The other kidney shut down, and he wound up staying in the hospital for almost a week while I danced. The next year, Rick had serious personal problems because of sexual abuse that he experienced during the Longest Walk, and by then we'd moved to Northern California. Dennis Banks and others in AIM didn't acknowledge what had happened to Rick, and Rick just slowly backed away from that organization. He didn't want anything to do with AIM, or even with Sundance any more.

Lushanya began dancing when she was three. She danced on the fourth day to give the dancers strength as they completed their fourth day of dance. Children often do this to help a relative who is dancing. Children are not expected to fast and are given fluids throughout the day. She and Tiopa, Dennis Bank's little girl, who was about Lushanya's age, danced the last day. I remember it was very hot and Dennis had asked me to give the girls something to drink, so in-between every round I would take them to the teepee and give them water or some lemonade, and at one time I even gave them some oranges, to see them through the day. When they got tired, we would have them sit and rest under a tree. They wanted to do what they saw their moms doing, but they didn't understand why they were doing it. I knew that. Dennis knew that too. Lushanya danced for four years, on the fourth and last day. She liked it. It wasn't until she got older and she'd pledged to dance four days that she found it hard. But Lushanya is Sundancing still to this day. In the end, it's important for our kids to get that exposure, but ultimately they must make up their own minds about the path they're going to follow.

A HOSPITAL VISIT TO MY SON RICK

It was about a hundred and fourteen degrees in South Dakota. I still was very naive about protocol and when they rushed Rick to the hospital after he collapsed and his kidney shut down, I wasn't allowed to accompany him. But later that evening, I had to go the hospital so I could sign the papers giving permission for him to be treated. They had one of the older dancers, Anna, drive me to town, a woman who had danced for several years. We drove into town and went to see my son. We watched him drink big cups of ice water. It was excruciating.

When we got back into the car to get back to the Sundance, Anna said, "Man I could use a cup of coffee and a donut."

In California, they had these coffee shops called, Winchell's Donuts, similar to Dunkin Donuts. I said, "Yeah, that would be good, but we're fasting."

She said, "What do you think Ellen and all the leaders are doing right now? They're all sitting around eating."

I thought, wow. So, we went to Winchell's Donuts, and we each got a cup of coffee and two donuts. I picked up a donut but then decided I'd drink my coffee first. I picked up my coffee and just had it to my mouth when the woman behind the counter said, "What's going on? I noticed all these Indian people coming in here with these little red marks on their arms—what is that?"

Our flesh offerings? That's what she saw. I threw my coffee across the room, jumped up, and ran outside. Anna was right behind me. We left the donuts behind. We got in the car and took off. It was as though we had been caught. It was comical, actually. Anna was a senior dancer who was supposed to be teaching me. We did stop at a gas station and I washed my hair in the sink, because I couldn't stand it. Since we were not able to even sneak breaking our fasts, I guess we thought that washing up when we should not be bathing made up for it. So much for adhering to tradition.

In those early years, there was no one to guide me. There was no one to tell me what was expected, what was not, what I was allowed to do, and what I wasn't allowed to do. And then, all the reasons for the protocol.

LAUNDRY DAY AT MY FIRST SUNDANCE

The main reason I had no one to guide me was because I was living in Los Angeles, far from Green Grass where the Sundance was held. I talked to my cousin Archie—who was a Sundance leader—about what was happening and asked him what I needed. I knew basically nothing.

He told me I needed to have a dress and a shawl. The first year I showed up with two dresses. I didn't know we wore the same dress all the way through. It was hot and we were all dusty and miserable. In addition to the heat we had to deal with a million mosquitoes. I was being eaten alive by mosquitoes and nothing I did could stop the discomfort. On the third night, one of the women working in security—they had security posted around so the dancers couldn't leave or no one could come into the dancers' area (which I always thought was a little odd)—said she was going to do some laundry. Not knowing any better, I gathered up all my underwear, my sweat things, and my Sundance dress and gave them to her. Next morning after the sweat lodge, everybody was getting ready and I was waiting for my dress. I was waiting for Ramona to come down the road and Ellen Moose Camp said, "What are you waiting for, Beverly? Go get dressed."

I said, "Well, Ramona has my dress."

She said, "How did Ramona get your dress?"

I said, "She was going to do laundry, so I gave her my dress to take to the laundry."

You could have heard Ellen scream ten miles away. Just about then Ramona drove up, jumped out of her car, and brought my things over to me. I ran inside the teepee and hurriedly pulled on my dress. Ellen said, "I want you all to know, your sisters here have been suffering here for three days, but Beverly's got a clean dress on." It was awful. I was mortified.

MY LEARNING YEARS AT D-Q

Each year I learned a little bit more. I was one of a few Lakota women when we moved to D-Q. Within the treaties of California Indians, it says that any government facility that's no longer in use should revert back to the Native people. So the California tribe wanted to reclaim that prime piece of property in order to establish a college, an institute of higher learning. They were in the process of cleaning it up because it had been trashed and they were recruiting qualified educators to teach subjects relevant to Native people. As I said earlier, Dennis Banks wasn't allowed to go back to South Dakota because of the governor's threats on his life, and he had been told to dance where he was. As I lived in California, it made all the sense in the world that I should support him in California instead of going to South Dakota. As a Lakota, I was constantly being asked to do things—like to stand at the head of the person who was being pierced, to pray with him, to bring the pipe. My teacher was my cousin, Archie Fire. His son, John, had his ear pierced at Sundance and I was the one who did it. I somehow ended up in the role of guiding the other dancers without anyone ever asking me directly if I would like to do it. I think they thought I should do this because I am a Lakota woman. Those years at D-Q were a training ground of sorts and I learned a lot.

The tree they use in the centre of the arbor serves as the altar and

Sundance arbor, 1999

represents our Mother Earth. It is always cottonwood. The men would have to go out and find it. It had to be forked at a certain juncture, and it was not allowed to touch the ground. It had to be carried to the arbor. I never understood why women who were on their moon cycle were not allowed to be nearby when the tree was picked; they wanted a virgin to make the first cuts. No one was ever able to explain this to me, although I asked the question several times. I would often be the one standing there holding the pipe while they got the tree and prepared it. I remember watching, and thinking, oh, I don't have to pay attention to what the men are doing. I'm never going to do that. That's not my role. I saw a lot at D-Q, too, and there was a lot I didn't feel was right.

RICE FIELDS AND MOSQUITOES

Besides the land the college was going to be built on, and Sundance grounds, D-Q had rented or leased another large portion of land to a rice farmer. Between the women's teepee and the men's teepee there was a huge pile of Deep Woods and Off to prevent mosquito bites. Now, while the rice is growing, it provides an ideal place for the mosquitoes to colonize. And they didn't have to go far for food. Just over the fence to where we were. And boy, did they get a lot of food from me. I was determined to find something natural that I could use to keep them away from me. The next year someone suggested Penny Royal, an herb that is a member of the mint family. I bought Penny Royal, which is very expensive, and they still ate me up. The next year I tried eucalyptus. That didn't work either. Then someone said, try Avon Skin-So-Soft. I thought, how silly, that's a moisturizer for your skin. I bought Avon Skin-So-Soft, and unless you're applying it every two minutes, the mosquitoes still eat you up.

The next year I tried garlic. Yes, it was the year of the garlic bulb. I had read somewhere that if you had a lot of B-vitamins in your system, the mosquitoes wouldn't bother you, and the best way to get the B-vitamin inside you was to eat raw garlic. So, I swallowed two or three bulbs of garlic, one clove at a time. I dipped them in butter and then swallowed them. The second day while I was dancing, one of the men said, "Man, I smell pizza."

I got really angry and said, "You're not here to be thinking about food, you're here to fast and to pray." I thought about it and then realized that I was the one who smelled like pizza; the garlic was permeating my skin! I thought, oh, my gosh. I thought, okay, I give up. Give me the chemicals. The next year, I went to the Army Surplus Store and bought Deet. Mosquitoes didn't bite me any more. Oh, they were horrible.

MY MOTHER COMES TO SUNDANCE

The year I bought the Deet was the year my mother and brother were taking a trip to South Dakota, and because I knew they would be coming through Sacramento, I asked them to stop and visit me at Sundance. I started dancing the first day and that afternoon I saw a little blue van coming down the road. My brother had a blue van, and I knew it was his. I saw the van make its way over to my teepee and I thought, oh, my mom's here. I waited for her to come to the arbor. They stayed for the entire day, but neither she nor my brother ever came to the arbor. They just stayed at my teepee. That evening, when we had finished dancing and I had come out of the sweat, security brought my mother over to talk to me. She said, "We're going to go. We're leaving. Your brother wants to get to South Dakota."

I said, "I was hoping you'd stay."

She said, "Well, I came over to tell you because I want you to come with us."

I said, "I think I could arrange that. I could get someone to watch the kids. Do you want to leave on Sunday or Monday?"

She said, "No, we want to leave tonight."

I said, "But I'm not through dancing "

She said, "I don't know what they're doing here. They've got flags, the colours are all different. They've got them in different places. I don't think this medicine man knows what he's doing. There are more songs than just those two songs that they sing." She was tearing the whole ceremony apart.

I said, "Mom, I really want to go with you to Grandma's. Can you wait for me just one more day?"

She said, "Who do you care more about, these people here or your mom?"

I said, "Well, you, Mom. My family's important."

She said, "Well, then, come on."

I said, "I can't."

After arguing for a while longer, my mother turned around and started to walk away. Archie Fire had been standing there listening. He looked at me and said, "You know, you don't have to stay. You can go."

I shook my head. "No, I don't have that choice. I have to stay."

He said, "Well, you decide what you're going to do."

I was crying. I turned around, ran back to the teepee, grabbed my sleeping bag and everything else, dropped it all into a big pile, and then ran out of the teepee. I ran to the perimeter and saw the the tail lights of the van as it was backing out. Archie said, "I can call the security gate and have them hold the van so that you can go."

I said, "No. I have another day to dance for my family, for the people, for Mother Earth, for the Creator." I turned around and walked back into the dancer's teepee and cried myself to sleep.

My mother told me just before she died how proud she was of me that moment, how proud she was of me for not giving in to her, for staying to dance. I thought, boy, that sure was a hard way to show it. She simply said, "I'm proud of you for not coming."

HOMOPHOBIA IN THE SUNDANCE COMMUNITY

There were many times at Sundance that gay women would come. There were many gay men who also came. Always, there were many homophobic remarks, jibes, and so-called jokes. One year, we had an International Treaty Conference at D-Q. People came from all over. A group of women came from San Francisco from an organization called Gay American Indians. They had a table with all kinds of literature on it. We always had security at D-Q; I guess they were protecting Dennis Banks, though I'm not quite sure what that was all about. Security went up to Gay American Indians' table and swept all the materials into a trash can. Then they physically dragged the women at the table—one of them was an Elder—out the gate and onto the road. They told them to go away and not to come back.

I encouraged a couple of them to write letters to Dennis and to the Board, and they did. Dennis made an eloquent speech about how he would gladly and proudly wear a pink triangle in solidarity with his gay brothers and sisters, and that our struggle was one and the same. This speech was written in response to a white organization who'd sent him a letter protesting the treatment of Lesbian and Gays at D-Q after hearing about what happened. Native women from the Gay American Indians organization had also written him a letter and they never got a response. That spoke louder to me than anything else.

A man named Bill Wakapa would speak at La Pena Centre in Oakland. He would talk about the solidarity between Native people and the gay and lesbian community—about the struggles that we all had—and profess deep solidarity. Then he'd go to a restaurant, sit down with members of the Native community who were straight, and poke fun at gays. While it made me sick, I was still terrified to say anything about being gay. I was afraid to defend them or to speak up on their behalf because I might have eyes cast my way. It was not a comfortable feeling. It was not a feeling I enjoyed having. I went to San Francisco and participated in the Gay and Lesbian Pride Day Parade held there each year to celebrate the Lesbian and Gay community, and I helped carry the banner at the front of the group. Every step I took, I was terrified that someone would recognize me. Being in the closet is a horrible thing, especially when you see the rest of the world around you having the courage to do something that you don't have the courage to do.

I had danced at D-Q for as long as I could dance. The Sundance there ended around 1984 when Dennis left California and went to Onondaga, undercover, and wearing a blond wig, driving across the country in the back of a van. He made an ugly woman. They drove into Onondaga and he was able to seek refuge on their reservation with his family. At that point, he stopped doing the Sundance in California and we took the Sundance back to Wambli, in South Dakota. I saw that as a good thing because more Lakota were able to get involved. The politics at D-Q were getting so convoluted that it didn't seem to be a sacred place anymore. And the mosquitoes, by the way, were also getting really bad. There were politics in South Dakota, too, within the dancers and within the community. I was surprised by that because I expected more cohesiveness.

CIRCLE OF ABUSE IN A LESBIAN RELATIONSHIP

Then I met a woman named Charlene and everything changed. I met Charlene at Sundance, 1984. Rooster, her brother—his real name is Darrell—had been in a car accident and had brain damage. He was having seizures and severe health problems and Charlene was there to offer prayers for him, to help him. The brain damage really affected Rooster. He worked at the post office still, but you could tell he was differently-abled. He was a big guy and he had long, long hair. He would get up early in the morning and walk through Sundance camp, crowing, singing "Cock-a-doodle-doo, cock-a-doodle-doo, time to wake up!" That's how he got nicknamed Rooster. Rooster carried this big metal cup for coffee. He'd go into a restaurant and say, "I want a cup of coffee," and they would bring him a little cup. He'd say, "No, I want it in my cup," and he'd hand them his big metal cup. He came to Sundance that year with his mother and Charlene, his youngest sister, who had a six-year-old son. Charlene and I became friends. She and her mother wanted me to visit them in Phoenix some time after Sundance. I flew out there alone and spent about a week with them. Charlene and I spent a lot of time together just sightseeing and talking. It wasn't a romantic relationship. We were just friends. Even though I knew I was lesbian, I didn't know how to tell her. I was afraid I'd lose her friendship if I came out to her.

Before the next Sundance, Charlene and her mother came to visit me in California. They also stayed for about a week. We spent a lot of time together preparing meals and taking my kids and Charlene's son to the park. It was her mom's sixty-second birthday, so we had a little bash for her. I realized that I was very attracted to Charlene. I kept pushing that feeling down because I assumed she was straight and I didn't want to overstep my boundaries. I finally decided that I needed to tell her that I was a lesbian. We were at the river. The kids were playing in this little pool area that was sectioned off in the river. I started talking to her about my feelings for women. I said, "I guess what I'm trying to tell you is that I'm gay, and I'm really, really worried that I'll lose you as a friend." That was met with dead silence. I kept looking at her, expecting her to say something. She was chewing on a blade of grass and never said a word. Finally, I said, "Well, maybe we'd better get to the store so we can go home and get dinner started."

She said, "Okay," but never said a word about what I had just said to her. I wondered, did I really say it? Did I only say it in my mind? Why was there no response?

A few days later, Charlene and her mom left. I went back to my life. Charlene would call every morning. She'd been doing this for some time. She would call and we'd talk. At the time, I had two jobs. During the day, I worked I took care of an elderly woman, and in the evening, I worked at a local nursing home. One day, while I was getting ready to go to my evening job, I got a phone call. Charlene said, "We're up in Oregon. We're on our way. We should be at your house by this evening."

I said, "Oh."

She said, "Yeah, we came to a Sundance up here, but it wasn't what we expected so we're on our way back down.

I thought, oh, and I said, "So, how long are you staying?"

She said, "I don't know."

I said, "Well, I'll be at work but come on in and make yourselves at home. Kenny, my husband, will be here."

She said, "Okay."

So that evening when I stepped out the door expecting my husband to be there and pick me up, Charlene was there instead with her van. She said, "I told Kenny I'd pick you up."

I said, "Oh, well thanks."

She said, "Have you eaten?"

I said, "Well, yeah, I ate at around seven. That was my dinner."

She said, "Well, I brought some sodas." She had these big slurpee-type sodas that she had just bought at the convenience store. She said, "Could we just go for a drive?"

I said, "Sure, do you want to go up to the dam? It's a place I used to go and I'd sit there. You can see the whole city. It's peaceful."

So we drove up to the dam. On her prior visits she had told me about this man who'd asked her to marry him. She didn't love him, but she was considering marrying him just so she'd have someone who'd take care of her. I cautioned her against doing that. "You know," I said, "it's hard, but you don't know him well and you don't know what you're getting into, so if you're not in love with him, don't risk that."

I asked her what was going on with that man and she said, "Oh, it's all over. I told him there was no chance."

I said, "Well, it's too bad you couldn't have maintained a friendship." She just shrugged.

Then she got out her seashell and started burning a handful of cedar in it. I thought she was going to build a little bon fire to roast hot dogs or something because she was burning a lot of cedar and a lot of sage. She turned to me and said, "I really need a hug."

I said, "Oh, okay," and I spun my chair around to face her—it was a van with these captains' chairs that swivelled. I reached over and hugged her and she just hung on. She was clinging to me like an octopus. As I tried to pull away, my cheek brushed against hers. The next thing I knew, we were locked in a very deep kiss. I was horrified, totally horrified. When I managed to break away, I apologized profusely. I said, "I'm so sorry. I didn't mean to do that and I'm really sorry."

She just smiled and said, "It's okay."

I was baffled. She got up, took me by the hand and moved to the back of the van where there was a couch that had been made into a bed. She started kissing me again. We wound up in the back of that van, making love all night, and until the sun came up. She said she had never been with a woman before. I was thinking, wow, you sure know a lot for not ever having been with a woman before. In the morning we went back to the house. Kenny was up. I said, "We sat up talking all night." I knew I was head over heals in love with her. I had a small fan I'd made out of individual eagle feathers. I went to my altar and prayed, burning sage. I took that fan and gave it to her. From that moment on, we were inseparable. Her mother found out and said, "Kenny's going to kick your butt." Charlene told her mom, "I don't care."

Every chance we got, we were together. When we got ready to go back to South Dakota for Sundance, she said, "Let's go in my van. We can all go together." So, we went cross-country from California to South Dakota with Kenny driving, my one son sitting up front and my daughter and Charlene's son sitting behind them, and she and I sitting in the very back. Sometimes we lay down and made love while Kenny was driving. Very quietly. He was oblivious. At least he never let on.

ONE WAY MIRRORS

One of the most embarrassing moments in my life occurred on that trip. We got to Rapid City. We were on our way to Pine Ridge, about eighty-five miles away. We had all this laundry and we had to do all this grocery shopping. First, we loaded the machines at a laundromat and then left my son, Charlene's son and my daughter and my husband there to watch the laundry. In the meantime, we said we'd be doing the shopping at the grocery store to expedite time. We bought all the groceries, put them away in the van, then pulled into the municipal centre's parking lot—a huge parking lot. There were no other cars around us. Charlene and I took off our clothes and made love in the back seat of that van. A car drove into the parking lot and circled us several times. We thought they were probably wondering why a van with Arizona plates was in the parking lot. Afterward, we went back to the laundromat, picked up Kenny and my son, and went on out to the Sundance grounds to set up the teepee.

Two days later we were cleaning out the van, trying to get things in order. Charlene said, "Beverly, look at the van."

I looked at it and said, "Yes, okay, it looks nice."

She said, "No, look at it. Look in the back windows."

I stood there looking at the back and said, "It looks good. You cleaned it well." All of a sudden it dawned on me that the shades that were on the windows were the kind that you could see out of, but from the outside you could not see inside. The kids had knocked the shades down during the trip, and then put them back up backwards—so we couldn't see out, but everybody else could see in.

Now I know why that car was circling us. I never want to go back to Rapid City again!

THE FINAL DAYS OF MY MARRIAGE

The Elders at that Sundance ask the women to wear skirts to the arbor. That was my first clue that Charlene was really obstinate. Wearing a skirt was not a problem for me, but Charlene refused to wear a skirt. I was in the arbor after having finished a round of dancing, and taking a break, when Charlene sat down right outside where the dancers were. She was finally wearing a skirt, but she was also wearing shorts under her skirt, to show me she was still wearing pants. At that Sundance, she had pledged to dance. She danced one day, though, and she said it was too hard, that she had to quit. We told her we'd give her juice, and do whatever she needed to keep her there, but she was done. She said she couldn't dance anymore.

When it came time to leave, Charlene took all of my husband Kenny's belongings and put them outside in a pile on the ground. We were driving out and just as we got near the gate we saw Kenny standing there with a bunch of guys and they were shooting the breeze. He saw us and said, "Oh, you're ready to go."

I said, "Yeah, we're all loaded."

He said, "You got all my stuff in there?"

I said, "No, if you want your things, they're back in the camp in a stack."

He said, "Oh, well, I'll go get them."

I said, "No, Kenny. I'm not taking you back to California with me. This is it. It's over."

He started saying, "I was really looking forward to going back this time. I am going to buckle down and do what I'm supposed to do."

I said, "Uh-uh." We left and travelled to California alone. When we got there, the phone was ringing off the hook. Kenny had been calling. He'd somehow gotten down to Kansas City and he called to tell me that Philip Deer, a Muskogee medicine person, was ill. I knew that he was ill and I knew that the end was clearly coming. Kenny said, "Beverly, Philip is really in a bad way and if you want to see him again, you probably should get here ASAP." I thought it was just a ploy to get me there, but Philip had indeed taken a turn for the worse and he did pass.

By the time Kenny came back to California, I had sold everything, loaded up our personal things and moved to Arizona. Charlene had insisted that she was buying a house in Phoenix and we wanted to live together. I thought that would probably be a good thing because the town I lived in at the time was very small. So, we drove to Phoenix. Once after being there a few weeks while I was driving, all of a sudden some guy on a bike cut in front of me. I almost ran him over and then realized it was Kenny. I pulled over and confronted him. He said, "I'm your husband. We're married."

I said, "We are married, you can get a divorce if you want to, but I don't want to be with you any more."

He said, "Well, that's not fair. If it was a man you were with, at least I'd know how to handle that, but I don't know how to handle it when you're with a woman."

I said, "Well, you'll figure it out."

I had put all my things in storage in Southern California when we left to go to Phoenix. I had no idea we had no place to stay. I was assuming that when we got to Phoenix there'd be a place waiting for us. When we went out to Charlene's house in Chandler, it was all locked up. Charlene found an open window, pushed her son through, and we got in that way. The house was completely empty. There was no furniture in it whatsoever. Charlene said her mother must have put the house on the market. She couldn't have sold it, though, because it was in Charlene's name as well as hers. Then we found out the next day that her mother had moved out, put everything in storage, sold a lot of their mutual stuff, and was now living up in Winslow. So we unloaded some of our stuff into the house and decided we would stay there for a couple of days. We didn't have running water, but we'd rough it, camping with four walls around us.

Then Charlene's mother showed up early one morning with Charlene's older sister. I woke up to the sounds of yelling and hearing the sounds of flesh connecting. I walked into the hallway and Charlene was pummelling her mother and her mother was hitting back. They were having a fist fight. I quickly scooted between the two of them, pushed them apart and said, "Stop this." They told me to mind my own business.

That day I went out and found a place to rent. Charlene was livid when she found out I had done that. I said, "You can come with me or you can stay here, but I'm not going to live with that kind of violence."

She said, "I don't want to live with it either."

I thought, you're contributing to it, even if you don't want to live with it. I had called a friend and borrowed some money for the rent. We found a little house and we moved into it. At this time, I had only two of my children with me, Alexx and Lushanya. I also had a cat and two dogs. The house wasn't near a busy street, but I knew the dogs weren't city dogs so they couldn't run around. We put them in the back yard, fenced in. The little dachshund's name was Tootsie and Alexx was very attached to Tootsie. Tootsie got out one day and Alexx found him two blocks away and on the street, dead. Alexx was hysterical. Poor, poor Alexx.

No sooner had Tootsie died than Charlene's son Ben didn't come home from school one day. We went looking for him and found him in a tree he had climbed to hide in. We found out from his teacher that Ben had found his way out onto the street. When I found him, he had this huge toy—a forty-dollar toy—in his arms. I asked him where he got the toy. He told me he'd bought it. I said, "Where?" And he pointed to a store. Then I asked, "Where did you get the money to buy it?"

He said, "I sold my school paper and pencils."

I said, "You would have had to sell them for an awful lot to be able to buy this forty-dollar toy." Finally I said, "You stole it, didn't you?"

He said, "Yeah."

I said, "Okay." I marched him back to the store and I made him find the manager, admit that he had stolen the toy from the store, and return it. The manager was sympathetic and said, "We're going to take your picture, and if anything comes up missing, we're going to call you." I don't know how much of an impression it made on him, but I used the same tactic with all my children. I never spanked them, but got them to admit what they had done, told them it was wrong, and then showed them what the consequences could be.

THE BEGINNINGS OF PHYSICAL AND VERBAL ABUSE

About three days later, it was Ben's birthday. We didn't have very much money, so I bought a cake mix and some eggs and I baked him a cake. He came in the house with a brand new pair of grips for his bicycle with little fringes and pompoms. I said, "Those are very nice."

He said, "I bought them with my own money."

I was kind of taken aback and I thought, maybe he had money that I wasn't aware of, so I didn't say anything. I thought about it for a few minutes and then asked, "Where did you buy them?"

He mumbled something about a sporting goods store and then said, "I didn't buy them, my friend bought them. He gave them to me for a present."

I said, "Why don't you give me your friend's number and I'll call, just to be sure that his mother is aware that he did this." The price of the fringes and pompoms was about sixteen dollars and for a six-year-old, that's a lot. Of course, he hemmed and hawed about it just enough that I knew he wasn't telling the truth.

Charlene started screaming at me about not trusting him and not believing him. That he'd stolen something once and that it didn't mean he would steal for the rest of his life. I said, "I know that, but I just have this gut feeling." So, she and I weren't talking. Later, there was a knock at the door and it was the other little boy's mother. It turned out Ben had stolen the fringes and pompoms. After the woman left, I got up and went into the bedroom. All of a sudden Charlene burst through the door. I stood up and turned to her. That quickly, she punched me right in the face, pushed me back on the bed, kneed me in the stomach, and then kneed me some more. I should have walked out then. We had been together six weeks. But I didn't. Of course, the next day, she was remorseful and said she was sorry. I was terribly upset. "It won't happen again, I promise," she said. That was the beginning of the physical violence and abuse.

There were other things. Charlene would get angry if we went somewhere and someone paid a little attention to me, or was nice to me, or it looked like we might become friends. She would start beating on me for that. One day, I told her I'd had enough and I was leaving. She went into the bathroom and swallowed a whole bottle of theophylline. She had asthma. Theophylline is asthma medication. She came out of the bathroom and she threw this bottle of theophylline at me. "I hope you're happy," she said. I very firmly took her by the shoulder, marched her out to the car, and drove her to Indian Health Emergency Room. I told them about the theophylline.

While we were driving to the emergency, she kept telling me that, no, she hadn't taken all those pills, yet when we got to the hospital and they pumped her stomach, it was clear that she had. She was livid because they made her swallow charcoal and pumped her stomach. They kept her there for three days. I visited her every day. When we got home, she admitted to me that she did it just to get my attention. Of course, she had my sympathy and I was right there for her.

We used to socialize with a group of lesbians who met each week to play games. We met in the basement of a local church in Phoenix. It was called Moon Tree. On Friday nights, they hosted a social hour for lesbians. We met a friend there and after Moon Tree was over, we were all going to go to a drag show. I had never been to a drag show and I really wanted to go. There was a gay club in town, so we were going to go there. I said, "We'll meet you there because I want to go home first to make sure the babysitter can stay a few hours later." On our way back to the house, Charlene started giving me the blues about this woman, our friend, saying that she knew I was attracted to her. I said, "She's just a friend."

Charlene said, "She doesn't look at you just like a friend."

I said, "I can't control how she looks at me, but I only see her as a friend."

Charlene went off on a tangent. She called me a slutty whore, and a bitch. I was shocked. My mom and dad didn't cuss. That was the one thing about them. The worst thing my father ever said was, "holy horse shit" or "holy sheep shit." My mother said "hell" every once in a while, but not very often. So when Charlene started with her four-letter words and they were directed at me, I was stunned.

I loved Charlene very much. At the time, she was the love of my life. She was a Native woman and I thought she was on the same path I was on. She had a child. I had children. I had prayed when I was coming out, about being lesbian, about whether it was right or wrong, about whether I was supposed to even come out. I prayed because in my relationship with my last husband, Kenny, the alcoholism was so prevalent, that all I wanted was a good relationship. I prayed, "Creator, if I'm meant to be lesbian and walk this path in this lifetime, then bring someone into my life who is at least part Native and who understands the way of the pipe and who, preferably has children and understands the responsibilities of a lesbian with children. And if that's not possible, then make me love my husband and let things get better with my husband." When Charlene came into my life, it was like she was the answer to my prayer. I just gave myself to her completely. I was totally in love with her. I wanted it to work. I knew that she had also been sexually abused as a child and that she also had her baggage, so to speak, and I thought if I loved her enough and if we got counseling, that she'd get better. But I wasn't prepared for physical abuse.

I said, "You know, I'm not going to do this. I'm not going to argue a few blocks from home." I pulled over off the busy street onto a side street. She got out of the car and started to tell me that she wasn't going to do it either, that she was fed up with me. She walked out on the middle of this four-lane city street and she lay down. I screamed at her to get up. I didn't want her to get killed or get hurt. It was a fight to get her onto the sidewalk. I thought, that's it, I'm leaving her. When she was safe, I got back into the truck and started to drive. She started chasing the truck and tried to hang onto the bumper, almost being dragged. I finally stopped the truck and she got back in.

At home, she would verbally abuse me and every time I'd start to fall asleep, she'd start slapping me or hitting me. I barely slept at all. By morning, I'd be exhausted. I still didn't see that as abuse. I saw it as her being so lonely and so afraid that I was going to leave her. This went on for four years.

I knew I needed to leave, but somehow I couldn't find the courage to do it because I loved her. I kept hoping she would change. I kept hoping she would love me enough to realize that the way she was behaving was not how you express love. I thought if I just loved her enough, it would stop. All those things women wo are abused tell themselves. I thought it was my entire fault. And then, the beatings got worse and worse. She would beat me for almost any little thing. And, I never went anywhere alone. When I went to nursing school, she would take me there, drop me off, come back at lunch time, pick me up. I never went to the store alone either. I was very controlled. It was a very controlled relationship.

FAMILY AND INDIVIDUAL COUNSELLING

We did get some counselling—also, because her son was having a hard time adjusting to being part of a blended family. He'd been an only child and he was very angry. One of the things that he became very angry about when we left California and returned to that empty house in Chandler was that all of his belongings— he'd had his own room—were gone. His grandmother had sold everything. Not only was his life changing—his mom was now with a woman, and we were a new family—he'd come back to an empty house. He'd been used to being with his mom and his grandmother, so he was grieving the loss of his grandmother, too. We would go to counselling and he'd just sit there. He wouldn't respond to anything. We couldn't talk to him. The therapist said, maybe he needs to come to counselling on his own. We tried to do that and he refuse to go. You can't force someone into counselling who doesn't want to go.

We went to a counselling session one day, and in front of the children, Charlene began complaining about me. She said, "She doesn't have sex with me enough. She's not being sexual with me." I was mortified because we were not there to talk about our sex life. That's not what we were there for. I wanted to bring up the physical abuse and I didn't know how to do that. I was afraid that if I talked about it, it would make her look bad, that she would be seen in a bad light, and I didn't want that to happen. I think the counsellor we saw was not prepared to deal with a lesbian relationship. I finally saw a therapist on my own, a lesbian therapist. When I told her what had happened, she told me she couldn't be my counsellor as long as I stayed with Charlene. "You need to leave her," she said. I wasn't ready to do that, so I just stopped going to see her. She wouldn't see me so I thought, okay, she's trying to break us up. I told Charlene and she said, "She must have the hots for you, that's why she's trying to break us up. That's very unethical of her." I thought, well, maybe that's what was going on. So I stopped going to see that therapist.

In the meantime, it got crazier and crazier at home. We'd moved a couple of times. I was trying to work and go to school. Charlene had told me before we got together that she was a respiratory therapist and I thought she had a profession. Later, I discovered that she had been a nursing assistant. Two of the patients she had worked with were on ventilators, but she really wasn't a respiratory therapist. She hated working in the hospital. Oftentimes, we were at the same job site together and I felt like I was being stalked because she was always with me, twenty-four-seven. I finally got a job where she couldn't get a job, in an alcohol treatment centre. Then she quit her job, and said that she didn't want to do that kind of work any more, that she wanted to pursue her art.

Charlene was an incredible artist. She signed up for art school, but never went to classes. She never even started. By that time, I had begun to notice other things. She had checked into a job that she found in the paper for an aerobics instructor and it had said that training was provided. As it turned out, you had to pay a fee to take these aerobic classes and after you completed your classes, you found your own group of people to teach and you were able to use their gym. It cost about a thousand dollars to take the classes so she never took the classes. But she wrote her mother a letter and told her mother that she was teaching aerobics. There were many times like that where she would exaggerate the truth. I didn't see it as being particularly honest and when I confronted her on that, she got really angry. It made me begin to wonder how much of what she said to me was true. Where's the truth here? Through all of that, I couldn't have a friend of my own. I couldn't go to the store alone. I couldn't do anything alone. It was like being a prisoner. And still, I loved her. I really loved her. I was caught in the cycle of abuse.

PORCUPINE QUILLS

A number of years ago I had a dream. An Elder had told me, "Once you have that dream, then you can work with porcupine quills." She had showed me how to clean quills and how to work with them.

It was about 1985 when I went back to South Dakota with Charlene. We got up very early one morning. We were loading up the truck and trying to tie my teepee to the top. Charlene asked me if I had ever put the teepee on top of the truck before. I said, "No, I've never had this truck before."

She was standing there watching me and said, "I don't know how to tie this on." So, I did it by myself. Then she said, "How are you going to tie the suitcase up there?" We had this big, blue suitcase. I asked her to pass it to me. She lifted it up and I tied it down too. I had spent a good part of the night before ironing. I had all my clothes in the suitcase. They were ironed and I had my bras and underwear flattened out so I could get more clothes into the suitcase. By the time we got everything done and were ready to leave, it was three in the afternoon.

We had to make one stop along the way. We made the stop and we said, okay, now we're ready to get on the road. We started up the road—they call it B-line highway—out of Phoenix, going up toward the White Mountains. We were driving along and we had the tape player blasting. All of a sudden, the kids—Lushanya and Ben in the back—started pounding on the window that opened into the front of the truck. We looked back and they were pointing to the road behind us. I looked out the window and at the rearview mirror, and saw all my clothes lying in the middle of the highway—way back—and the rope I had tied the suitcase with was flapping in the breeze. The kids were telling us that we had lost our stuff. So I turned around and drove back. Charlene jumped out of the truck and walked down the middle of the road, picking up all the clothes. She yelled, "I've got them," and walked back to us. I had pulled the truck over.

Now, I'd had the headlights turned on, the a/c going, the tape player was playing, and we had the doors open, so the inside lights were also on. Of course, we didn't have a suitcase; the suitcase was demolished. I took all the clothes from Charlene and stuffed them into plastic bags. I got up onto the roof and I retied everything down. I tightened the ropes and, finally, when everything seemed secure, we got back into the truck. It wouldn't start. The battery was dead. The tape player had started dragging, so I had turned it off. I had turned the a/c off, too, but I wasn't quick enough. So, there we were, at eight o'clock in the evening, sitting there, with a dead battery. Charlene got out of the truck and grabbed one of the cardboard covers that we used to put over the windows to keep the car cooler. On the other side of the cardboard, it said, "Please Call For Help." A truck drove by. Then it turned around, pulled over next to us, and the man inside asked, "What's the trouble?" We told him our battery was dead.

He had jumper cables, so he got our car started. We got back on the road and we thought, oh, this is really good. We're really doing well now. Finally. We laughed about it while we headed up the hill.

We got about half way up, when suddenly the traffic slowed down. We saw a bunch of emergency vehicles. We thought, oh no, somebody had an accident. A Winnebago had caught fire and it was sitting on the side of the road, completely gutted. The family was standing there, the police were there, and we thought, how sad. They were going on vacation and this had happened to them. Without a batting an eyelash, I reached over and grabbed the seashell that sat between me and Charlene. It had sage in it. I lit the sage, smudged, and said a prayer for the family. I then set it down. Charlene decided it was too hot, so she turned on the air conditioning. The breeze blowing on the shell caused the sage to flame up. I felt something warm on my leg and there were flames half way up my leg. I screamed, "We're on fire!" Charlene doused it with the bottle of water she had in her hand. So then, everything was all wet in the car and I thought, oh my god, I should turn around and go home.

We got to Snowflake, got out of the car, had dinner, then got the kids settled back into the car. By this time, it was about two o'clock in the morning. We drove along desert roads, flat roads, for miles. We had the tape player on again and all of a sudden, really quick, something jumped out on the road in front of us, and I heard a loud thud. I was going about ninety miles an hour. I said, "Oh my god, I hit something." It looked like a porcupine. I got hysterical because I use porcupine quills and to hit a porcupine, to kill a porcupine, is terrible for me. I cried hysterically.

Charlene grabbed the wheel and said, "Beverly, take your foot off the gas. Take your foot off the gas." About a mile and a half down the road, I finally brought the car to a stop. I was sobbing. I said, "I have to go back. I have to go back and offer tobacco."

Charlene said, "But it's ten miles back."

I said, "I don't care. I have to go back." So, I turned the truck around and I drove back, but I didn't see it. I thought, well, maybe I didn't hit the porcupine. I thought, I'll go back another couple of miles and if I don't see it, there's nothing I can do. Then, there it was. It was lying in the middle of the road. It was a big porcupine. I pulled the truck around so that that the headlights were shining on the porcupine. I got out and ran over to it. It was still breathing. I said, "Oh my god, she's still alive." And just as I said that, the porcupine took her last breath.

I thought, oh no, the clothes, the battery, the Winnebago, and now this? For the rest of the trip, that's the way it was. All these strange things kept happening. And we still didn't turn around and go back home. I kept feeling we should just turn around and go back home. We got to South Dakota, we were driving, and all of a sudden a bird flew right in front of us and hit the windshield. But I couldn't find it on the road anywhere. It just disappeared. I thought, you know, this is not going to be a fun trip. This is not going to be a positive thing. And it wasn't.

Such was my relationship with Charlene, like a one-way trip with laughs and anguish and signs we didn't pay attention to.

The death of that poor porcupine was an omen of things to come. I did not even gather any of its quills. We just moved it off the road and left tobacco for its spirit. I did not use quills in any of my work for four years after I hit my friend porcupine.

That was a lesson I never repeated.

8.

FROG SEEDS

S HORTLY AFTER WE MOVED to Arizona, I found a church that had two sweat lodges behind the church. A man named Ashley tended the fire and kept the lodges there. I'd known him for a number of years. Ashley said, "I'll do the fire and I'll be your fire keeper any time you want to come." So, every Friday, a group of us women would meet there and I would do a lodge.

Leonard Crow Dog came into town, and found out I was doing lodges there. He came to the lodge one Friday night and told Ashley, "Mary's going to run the lodge tonight—the women's lodge." We'd gotten there really early and I just had a bad feeling about it. So we went in. I'd had him put on extra rocks so there'd be hot rocks when Mary got there.

When she got there I said, "I understand you need to run a lodge for your family and we've heated it up for you."

Leonard was mad. The next day he took the lodge down because "that queer" had been in it.

HELPING A WOMAN THROUGH BREAST CANCER

For a while, we were going down to the river and doing full moon ceremonies rather than putting up a sweat lodge because we had no place to put it. We finally moved into a house with a yard where we could put up a lodge, and we began having a lodge there once a month. A lot of women in the community would come. There was a Native woman named Cindy who came often. It turned out that she'd been a babysitter for my children when my husband, Caesar, worked at the drug and alcohol rehab, only now she was grown up. At first I didn't recognize her and then she saw Caesar's picture and she said, "Oh, don't you remember me?" We became friends. She came to a full moon ceremony one night, where she met another woman named Cindy, who was really tiny. Cindy Domingiz had a little girl. You could almost see the electricity between them when they both got out of their trucks at the same time. They looked at each other and it was like watching a movie. A couple weeks later, big Cindy was saying things like, oh, I took Cindy here, I took Cindy there, we went to California, we did this and we did that. At one point she said, "You call me Cindy Straight Arrow and her Cindy Twisted Arrow."

I laughed and I said, "Cindy Twisted Arrow? Shouldn't that be Mrs. and Mrs.?" She started laughing and she said, "Well, yeah."

So, they became lovers. About six months after they became lovers, she began experiencing homophobia at the lodge she attended in California, around the same time she was diagnosed with breast cancer. She called me up at four in the morning on a Thursday and asked if I would run a lodge for her. I said, "Four in the morning?"

She said, "Yeah."

She came over and helped set the fire so all I had to do was get up in the morning and light it. It was just her and I, and on the fourth round, I looked up and I saw her lying in a casket, just as clear as day. I thought, oh, my gosh. I interpreted that vision to mean that if she didn't go and get medical help right away, that she wasn't going to make it. In a way, that was accurate. What I didn't know was that she'd found a lump, that she had a doctor's appointment that morning, and that's why she had wanted to do the lodge beforehand. They did a test and told her to come back for an ultrasound. That was a Thursday. The Monday morning they did a double mastectomy.

Cindy prepared to move back to California to be near her parents and medical care. She started arranging plane fare for me to come out there to do lodges and pipe ceremonies for her. I would fly out there on a Friday evening and come back on a Sunday. Before my trips to California to see Cindy, she had started talking to me about things she had heard and visions she had seen. I told her that I thought her teachers were coming, and that she might be going on a journey. She said, "I feel that way, but people keep telling me that, no, I'm going to get better." I counselled her to listen to her own heart rather than to what other people say.

On one of my visits, Cindy met me at the airport and the back of her truck was full with camping gear. She said, "I had this vision that you are supposed to take me somewhere to meet the spirits. I checked it out with a psychic and she said that a woman with the name that has the letter B in it is going to take me to the gateway."

I thought, I don't know what she's talking about. Yet, I answered, "The only gateway I know is up by Santa Barbara."

She said, "Okay, let's go." So, I drove her to Point Conception, which is considered the western gateway of the Chumash people. That's where they believe their spirits go. I camped up there one time during the occupation of Point Conception with the Chumash people when multinationals were trying to put the LNG site in, a liquid natural gas pipeline. In the process of doing excavations, the company discovered burial grounds and they were just going to plow them under. But, with support, the tribe managed to stop them. When Cindy and I arrived at Point Conception, we realized the land was now privately owned and they had a guard. If you were not on a guest list, you couldn't get there.

When in doubt, go eat is what I say, so we went to a Pea Soup Anderson's and we sat and had split pea soup, iced tea, and bread. I said, "Well, let's go back to the camp ground and just camp for the night. Tomorrow I'll figure out how to get to Point Conception." We headed back and halfway there, a word came into my mind—La Chappelle. I thought, now what does that have to do with anything? I said to her, "Have you ever heard of a beach called La Chappelle?" She said no, and I said, "Hmmm. It just came to mind. I don't know why." When we arrived at the campground, I was looking for a little envelope to put our registration inside. I looked behind a big bulletin board, and there was a note. The note said, *Decided it was too crowded here. Have moved to La Chappelle Beach*, and the note had directions. I came back with this note in my hand, copied it all down, got in the car and didn't say a word. I just started heading north again.

We got to the bottom of the hill where this beach was and the sign said, "Full." I said, "If that's where we're supposed to go, we'll get in," so we parked on the side of the road and started up this hill. Just as we got to the office, two cars pulled out. When we went up the gate, the girl said, "Oh, you're lucky. The camp that I'm going to give you already has a camp fire going." One of the campers in that group had gotten sick, so they had left, and that made the two spots available. We pitched our tent and went to sleep. Then, at about three o'clock in the morning, I heard a big crash. It felt like someone had shaken the tent. I came out of a dead sleep. Cindy woke up and asked, "Are the spirits here for me?"

I said, "No, no, it's just something four-legged that got into our trash."

THE PLANTING OF FROG SEEDS

Cindy and I started talking. I told her I'd had a dream not that long ago that I was standing on a bridge and before me lay a pond, a pond that went on for infinity—one pond after another pond after another pond—so I could see no end. Some of the ponds had lily pads with frogs sitting on them and some of the them had lily pads with no frogs. There was a woman standing next to me. She had long hair and she seemed very kind. I stood there and I was holding onto a little medicine bundle I used to wear. She said, "Are you ready to go to the spirit world?"

I said, "What do you mean?"

She said, "What part of the pond do you want to go to?"

I looked at her and I said, "You mean when I die I'm going to become a frog?"

She smiled and said, "Yes."

I laughed and said, "Then you mean the fairy tale about the princess who kissed a frog and he turned into a prince wasn't really a fairy tale?"

She said, "No, it wasn't."

I laughed and laughed. I said, "Boy, is somebody going to be surprised when they kiss me because I'm a lesbian." She just smiled. I stared at these lily pads for the longest time and I decided that there was one part of the pond that had lots of lily pads and no frogs. I said, "I want to go there because there's lots of lily pads but no frogs and I like creating community."

She smiled then turned around and said, "Okay." Then she noticed the little medicine bundle I was holding. The whole time we were talking, the bundle kept getting bigger and bigger and bigger, and by the time we reached this point, I was holding a gunnysack. It was full of avocado pits. She said, "What's that?"

I said, "Oh, these are the seeds I didn't get to plant. I was supposed to plant them while I was here, but I didn't get to plant them."

She said, "You can't go to the spirit world until you've planted them all."

I started crying and I woke up crying. Cindy was quiet for a while and then she said, "You're supposed to travel and you're supposed to plant those avocado trees, those frog seeds." When I die, promise me that you'll leave Charlene—and the abuse—and begin to plant frog seeds."

POINT CONCEPTION

The whole tent started shaking again and Cindy asked in a panicked voice, "Are they here for me?" I told her no. I got out of the tent and saw there were raccoons. I realized that we had left some food sitting out and the raccoons had made off with our eggs. It was after sunrise, so I went to the bathroom and decided to go to the ranger station. They had a big map. I saw that they called Point Conception "Government Point." "How do you get to that from here?" I asked the man working there.

He said, "There's a gate. You have to have permission." Bill Bixby owned part of the land and Marlon Brando owned some of it too. Several people owned it. He said, "In order to go out there you have to have the permission of at least one of them." When I asked how I could get in touch with one of them, he looked a bit surprised and said, "I'm sure there are fan clubs." Then when I asked him how to access a fan club, he looked even more surprised and he asked me, "Why?"

I said, "I have a friend who has cancer and we need to go out there to pray. Can you get there by the beach?"

He said, "Yeah, but it's part of the beach, too." I explained to him that I wanted to know if it accessed the land because there were big cliffs, and he again he said, "Yeah."

I went back and told Cindy and she was very excited, "Let's go!" was all she said.

I thought twice about it, though, "Can you walk? It's seven miles. Can you walk that far?" I asked her. Her answer was certain, but I wasn't so sure. She had had chemo several times. The cancer had spread to her lungs and I was concerned about her ability to walk. But I loaded the backpack with lots of food and lots of water and I thought, if I have to, I'll carry this all the way. Then all of a sudden, a car came racing up—almost ran us down, and the driver said, "Are you the gals who wanted to go up north?" We nodded. "To Point Conception, right? Well, I'm the head of security," he said and I thought, oh great, he's going to tell us we can't go. But instead he said, "I can let you in, but you have to be off the land by ten o'clock because we only allow so many people to be out there at night."

I turned to Cindy and said, "He said we can go out there and we have to back by ten p.m."

She said, "Well, we can do that!"

So, we drove to the gate—he'd given us the combination. We were able to drive right out there!

It was absolutely beautiful. We found a nice shade tree and sat down. Trees are hard to find out there, so it was amazing to find this little scrub. I left Cindy there making tobacco ties while I went and built a fire, made a little altar, and then proceeded to take my pipe and pray. We sat there all day. As the sun was going down, I took the pipe over to her and said, "Face the west and offer your prayer."

She said, "I know what I'm going to say."

She started to tell me and I said, "No. Don't tell me. That's between you and Spirit, not me."

She sat there for about an hour. She came back, her face tear-stained. She said, "I have two things to say. One is, you can't remain closeted all your life. You have to spread those seeds. And when I die, will you bring my ashes back here?"

I promised her I would.

When I was sitting at the altar and then again when she took the pipe, four times a feather came off of the altar. I'd tie it up again really tight and the wind would just lift it off again. I knew that she was going to go soon. I kept seeing head tumours. I thought, she doesn't have brain cancer why does that keep coming to mind? I brushed it aside. Cindy asked me, "So, what did the spirits tell you?"

I just looked at her and said, "That we all live until we draw our last breath."

And so, she began her process. We left for home soon after. We cried all the way. I remember we listened to one of Holly Nears new CDs, and we just cried. We cried and cried. When we got her back home, she said, "Remember your promise to leave Charlene when I die, and remember your promise not to let me die alone." Again, I promised.

Three days after our return home, they discovered that Cindy had three brain tumours. That was in October. I was doing a lot of travelling at that time in my life. Most of the time I managed to go alone while Charlene stayed at home with the children. I went to Woman Gatherings. I did ceremonies, pipe ceremonies, and sweat lodges. I knew I would drop everything when Cindy's time came. Some time in early December, she called me and told me that this woman was going to drive her to New Mexico and they were going to see a medicine man who was going to heal her. I cautioned her against that, but she went anyway. She gave the man a thousand dollars. He told her he had pulled out wires, broken glass, tin cans, and he had a pile to prove it. He'd pulled all these things out of her head and then said she'd been witched by someone. On her way back, she stopped at my place and we had a lodge for her. Afterwards, I helped her get into the bed they had for her in the back of her van. I gave her a hug and she said, "Remember your promises."

I said, "I won't forget." This was December tenth. On January first, I got a phone call that she had been in the hospital for three weeks. She'd had a series of massive seizures and they were returning her home to go into hospice. She was asking for me.

So within two hours, myself and three others jumped in the car and drove to California where we spent the next four days taking care of her. She was at her mom's house. We stayed there, taking turns sleeping on the couch. We bathed her, changed her, massaged her feet and her hands and her back, and just took care of her. Her parents would come in to talk to her. At one point her father came in and asked to talk to me. He looked so lost. "Are you Beverly Little Thunder," he asked, and when I said I was, he looked at me with such pain and said, "My daughter's Catholic and she's supposed to be buried in the Catholic cemetery. I understand she's asked you to do something different? To have her cremated and her ashes spread somewhere?" He insisted that she was going to be buried in a Catholic cemetery. That was their way, and that's as far as he would go with it.

The others were saying, "Beverly, you've got to convince him."

I said, "No. He's losing a child. I'm not going to try to convince him he's wrong."

On January sixth, we had a pipe ceremony. We included her in the pipe ceremony when we went around. As soon as the pipe was finished and we stopped singing, she took her last breath and died.

THE SELF-STARTING FIRE

At the Catholic Church, we set up an altar off on the side. The priest allowed us to do that. Afterwards, we went to Point Conception and did a ceremony for Cindy. We got permission to go out to the exact same place where Cindy and I had been in October. We took all the things with us that were important to her and would have gone with her if she had been cremated. Cindy had made tobacco ties throughout her illness and we gathered those and took them there. And her hair she had saved when she cut it.. We burned sage and had fabric there for people to make tobacco ties. Someone spoke about who Cindy was in our community. We had a pipe ceremony and prepared for the burning of the things that needed to be burned. I built this fire, and it wouldn't start. Several people tried to light it and everybody

Beverly picking white sage, 2011.

asked what do you need? Do you need newspapers? What do we have? It just wouldn't start. It was a dead, quiet day. No wind, which is unusual because the cliff about seventy feet away had about a hundred foot drop and then there was the ocean, so we were really jutted out towards the ocean. There's always a breeze at the ocean. But that day, there was none.

Finally, after what seemed like forever trying to get the fire to start, I stood there and said, "Okay, Cindy"—because she had a sense of humour—"What are you trying to do?" All of a sudden, a spiral wind came up, swirled around the top of the teepee-shaped logs, and the whole thing went up in flames, without a match even being lit. Some would say that there must have been some coal down there and the wind pulled it up. I think it was Cindy. Everyone there felt it was Cindy. I said, "Cindy isn't back there at the church, she's here."

We had a giveaway and we had we had a little feast in her honour. I felt like that was the best I could do, considering since her father didn't want her cremated and scattered. When he finally consented to cremation, he insisted her cremains be buried in the Catholic cemetery. The family needed a place to go and visit her and I told her sisters, "Here at Point Conception is where Cindy wanted her ashes scattered. When your parents pass, then maybe you can bring your sister's ashes here and scatter them." They agreed that that's what they were going to do. I understand a few years later their dad died, and then their mom died as well. Through the grapevine I heard that Cindy's sisters did take her ashes to Point Conception. I had known it would not be an issue for her sisters to remove her urn from the Catholic cemetery and I'm grateful they were able to honour, finally, Cindy's last wishes.

MY BREAK-UP

It was as if Cindy was there reminding me of my promise to her when we were up at Point Conception that day. Charlene spoke about Cindy that day. Charlene usually said all these terrible things when Cindy was alive and now that Cindy was passed, she was saying all these glowing things, like Cindy was her best friend. Cindy knew that Charlene didn't like her, knew the accusations that Charlene had made about her and I being lovers. I was really upset. Cindy was so sick and the accusations made me feel I had to see Cindy on the sly most of the time. I was tired of living my life in fear. Cindy was right. I began to make plans to leave and I began to save some money.

The dynamics of abuse between two women in the lesbian community is insidious. It's kept quiet and there's so much shame involved. And I was hooked. I was so in love. I was confused and worn down and so in love. But I knew I had to leave. I couldn't even be in a bar or a nightclub or go to a dance that she was going to because I was so afraid of her. So, I had long ago stopped going to social events. I had stopped being active and social in the community. I kind of withdrew. Like so many others leaving a situation like that, most of the times I hadn't talked to people or told them about the abuse. I was too embarrassed and too ashamed to do that. So it was news to a lot of people when they heard, and they would say, why didn't you tell us before now, and I would say, I was embarrassed. That was something that was hard for them to understand. It was hard for me too.

Walking away from Charlene was one of the hardest things I've ever done. The interesting thing was, as soon as I left her, all these women started coming out of the woodwork that she'd had affairs with. I realized that she had been projecting what she was doing onto me. It wasn't me who had affairs, it was her! That made me very angry because during the time that we were just becoming aware of AIDS and I was really concerned because she'd been with men in the past and so had I. In those days, we had to get checked every three months because it wasn't known how long the virus lived. Until I was with Charlene, every three months like clockwork I would go and get checked. I thought, and she's been with all these women? The enormity of it was truly sobering.

I understand now that abusive relationships are often the most difficult to break away from because of how the abuse cycle permeates every aspect of your life, and to say it wasn't easy to leave is an understatement. I loved Charlene, loved her dearly. I still love her, at least the memory of who she was. I don't know who she is now. Back then, when I finally got the courage to leave, I had very little support. My children didn't even support me. They thought I was just trying to break up the family. It was so hard to leave for so many reasons, especially because of our children, and because of Sundance.

Today we have reconnected, both different women than we were then. We are friends on a whole new level and I still love her. I guess true love never really dies it just changes form.

9.

WOMYN'S SUNDANCE

I LEFT MY HUSBAND in 1985 and in 1986, Charlene and I went to Sundance together. I had been a Sundancer for many years and I was a women's leader. Charlene had pledged to dance two days in solidarity for her brother, Rooster, who was having health problems. She was immediately turned away from the lodge and told that she wasn't wanted there. She came back to our teepee, crying. My heart was breaking for her. I said, "You made that decision. Your pledge is between you and Spirit. They can't tell you what to do. Are you going to let them tell you what to do?"

She went back and again, she was told to go away. She said, "No. I'm staying right here."

One by one, the women in the lodge berated her. Later, one of the woman said to me, "Beverly, if you had come in and wanted to dance, you would have been welcomed with open arms because we all knew you, but none of us knew this woman who was trying to emulate a man. That's what turned a lot of us off." At the time I thought, well, why would that make a difference? But that's where those women were at during that time.

When Charlene was told she couldn't dance, I sat in the camp and cried with her. I went and talked to Dennis, Banks. He was one of the leaders. I also talked to Komook, another leader and wife of Dennis Banks. They said, "If this was our home, you'd be welcome in our home any time. We have no qualms against you being gay. But our hands are tied here." They thought I had some control over Charlene and wanted me to ask her to back down. I said, "I can't do that."

Ellen Moose Camp—the woman who was heading the dancers that year because that position had now been taken away from me because of my sexuality—said, "You know, women like you and her are taken out into the desert and shot, so be glad you're getting away with your life."

Two of the women Elders afterward came and talked to us and told us to have a ceremony for our own kind. It was a tactful way of trying to get us out of there. The last day of Sundance, I got up, went to the lodge, came back to my tent, got dressed, and headed up to join them in the dance. I was stopped by security. I said, "If I can't go to the arbor, then you need to get me some rocks for this lodge. I'm going into the lodge again." When I came out of the lodge, I was devastated. I felt as though I didn't matter, that I was not a valuable part of my community, that nobody wanted me there, so I just started walking. I walked and walked and walked, following a ravine.

I don't know how long I walked. It was really hot. I was barefoot. I started to scramble up the sides of the ravine and I saw a rattlesnake. I froze. I hadn't realized I'd been walking on rocks until that moment. I'd been crying the whole time. I thought, come on, bite me. Bite me and let me die here. I reached out for the rattlesnake. I threw a rock at it, hoping to get it to strike. I thought if I could get the rattlesnake to bite me, I could just lie there and die of poisoning. Instead, it crawled away from me. I started chasing it and it just kept slithering away from me. Then it slithered up the side of the ravine, got to the top, stopped, and kind of looked back at me. I thought, is there nothing right I can do in the world? The rattlesnake won't even bite me. I started to climb up the creek bed and the snake left. I found myself on a level piece of ground. There was a pine tree in front of me. It was really hot, so I went over and sat down on the ground next to the pine tree. I lay down and fell asleep.

Someone calling my name woke me up, but I continued to lie there for a long time. I heard my name again. Whoever it was, was getting closer. I curled up into a ball. I wanted to become invisible. Then my Hunka brother, Stampede, came around the side of a bush. I heard him yell, "I found her!" A Hunka relative is one who is chosen and becomes more important than a blood relative. Stampede and I had been through a Hunka ceremony several years prior. He knew I was diabetic. Stampede told me that when he had seen me wander off into the brush, and did not come back, he got concerned. He reached into his bag and pulled out a bottle of water. He had some bits of apple and some granola or trail mix or something. He said, "Here, eat this." So I ate and drank some water. I was really thirsty. He said, "The tribal police are looking everywhere for you." I asked why. He said, "I was worried about you." I told him I was sorry and then started crying again. He held me for a long time. Finally, he said, "Come on. Let's go. Let's just go take down the teepee. Let's go home. Come home to my family, your family. You don't need to be here."

I said, "But it's not fair. It's not right."

He said, "I know that and you know that and there are people here that know that, but then there are people here that don't know that. We don't need to waste our time with them and you don't need to hurt yourself over them."

I got up and we walked the long way back.

When we got to his house, Stampede told me what he knew about our traditions about gay women and men, and that he was sorry there were people there that didn't understand that, and that didn't honour that. Charlene and I stayed with him for about a week. He was married to a woman named Lisa, whose father was a man named Darrell Standing Elk. Darrell was one of the men who made up the core group of that Sundance, Rich Moose Camp. Bill Wampapa was there and so was Dennis Banks. I got a phone call from Dennis about a week later. He asked me to come over. Charlene and I drove over to his place. He was living in Oglala by then and Komook his partner had had a baby boy. Komook and all of Dennis's kids were there. We went in and Dennis was lying on a bed in the bedroom. The girls were all on top of him, wrestling and playing around with him, and the baby was perched against some cushions on the bed. Komook was in the kitchen, cooking. We went into the bedroom and sat down on a couple of chairs next to the bed.

He started asking how I was and then said that he wanted me to know that he and Komook had no concerns with my being gay. Komook came into the room then and sat at the foot of the bed. She said, "You're welcome in my home any time, with my girls any time. I've known you for a while and I know who you are."

Dennis said, "The important thing to me is the person you are, not who you are partnered with. Who you love is your business."

We talked for a long time. I left feeling comfortable with Dennis, though I remembered another time in another place, when I heard him telling someone that he, and all of AIM, supported gay people. That time, after the gay people left, he and the others made a lot of derogatory remarks about homosexuality, so I wasn't quite sure.

When we left South Dakota that summer after Sundance, I was feeling like I was leaving home for the last time. I never went back. Before I left, I said to Stampede, "I will not come back here and dance until the day all gay men and lesbians are welcome at all Sundance's. I have no need to be in a place where we are not honoured, we are not respected. I've lived too much of my life in the closet, pretending to be someone I'm not."

I could have gone to the Sundance and I could have danced and not said a word. They knew Charlene was Rooster's sister. They would have accepted her dancing as Rooster's sister. But when we said that we were partners, suddenly, did we grow horns? Did we suddenly turn into predatory monsters? I was the same person that I always was. The chokecherries that lined that arbor were the same chokecherries that I went out, that I cut, and that I stripped. The same chokecherries that I painted, that I put the ties on, that I drove all the way from Arizona to South Dakota to help with. They didn't turn those away. Those weren't tainted. Stampede agreed with me.

DREAMS OF A LIVING ARBOR

When we went back to Arizona, I began praying every day about what had happened. About a month later, I began to dream about a dance. There were women of all colours, all races, and they were Sundancing around an immense tree. There were tobacco ties all over the tree and all around the arbor. It wasn't an arbor I had seen before. There were two concentric circles of trees forming the arbor. I was very happy in that dream. I thought about what the Elders said to me in South Dakota. I continued to have the same dream at least once a week and after about four months, I thought, I need to dance where I'm at. I need to have a Sundance wherever I am, because I've made that pledge.

THE BEGINNINGS OF WOMYN'S SUNDANCE

Around that time, we became friends with a woman named Carolina, who was from Nicaragua. She was considered a Cunedera. We learned that Carolina had forty or fifty acres in the desert in St John, in the northeastern part of Arizona. She'd asked if I would come and perform a wedding ceremony with the pipe for her and her partner. During the wedding—there were about twenty or thirty women gathered—the subject of the Sundance came up, and I told them about the homophobia we had experienced. I explained to the women, "This year I am going to dance alone. Even if I have to tape the songs on a tape recorder and go somewhere out in the desert and dance for four days alone, I am still going to offer my prayers."

One of the women said, "If you teach me the songs, I'll come and drum for you and sing."

Another woman said, "I'll come and keep fire for your lodge."

Then the newly-married couple, Zelema and Carolina, offered, "You can do that here." So, we began making preparations for Womyn's Sundance.

The first year of Womyn's Sundance, 1987, I put an ad in the *Lesbian Connection*, a national lesbian newspaper, informing Native women, two-spirit women, about the Sundance. I had responses from everywhere. That first year one hundred and thirteen women came to the Sundance. Twenty of the women were Native and the rest were non-Native. A white woman had arrived on Zelema and Carolina's land two weeks before the dance. She had cut all of the posts for the arbor and had dug the holes to put them in all on her own, all by hand. When we got there, the rest of us helped with whatever was left to do. Everybody camped out—there was no structure that we could

Sundance teepee, 2009.

stay in. We put up a teepee. I don't remember if we had a large drum that first year. I know we didn't have the drum we use now. One woman came who remembered me from Green Grass in 1973. She was married to a man at that time. She sang by the drum back then and remembered some of the songs. She said she would be willing to drum for us. Everything seemed to be falling into place.

One day, from sunrise to sunset, I sat in the lodge and prayed alone. After the arbor was built and covered, I asked women not to walk past the East gate. It was hard because the way the arbor was situated; to get from point A to point B, you had to walk quite a bit out of your way to avoid the East gate. We are taught that the East gate of the arbor is the portal for the spirits to enter. During ceremony, only the dancers enter through the East gate. No one else is permitted to cross the opening. A few of us marked off an area and all of a sudden, as we looked down, a rattlesnake slithered into the arbor from the East gate. It climbed the tree, circled the trunk, then came back out the east gate, went over and into the sweat lodge, then came out and slid quietly away. We were all amazed! I remembered the rattlesnake that wouldn't bite me. I knew that was my sign, and that I was doing what I needed to do.

That first Sundance was not without its struggles. We had no kitchen. All we had was a very small—maybe four by eight—Ramada, a shade made out of two-by-fours and covered to provide actual shade. Someone had hastily put the Ramada up with some scrap lumber, and in there we had a little counter we used as a table. We had a little cook stove and an open fire. We had no way of keeping things cold. I think we had one ice chest.

One of the first Sundance kitchens, 1990.

A woman named Moon came with her VW. She worked with herbs, and she offered to be our cook. She was a vegetarian. I remember I asked her to make me a beef stew because a lot of the women there weren't vegetarian. We went into town and bought beef for that evening. We were still in preparation days before the Sundance started, and we had to eat. When I get to working really hard, I tend not to eat. Fortunately someone finally said, we need to sit down and we need to eat. Moon said, "I made a stew." I sat down and in the dim light of the lantern we had, she handed me a bowl and I started eating. I looked down and I saw these little white things floating and I thought, oh my god. The stew was full of maggots. The meat must have gone bad and Moon didn't know any better and cooked it up anyway. But it wasn't maggots. Moon had added a type of seaweed. I don't like seaweed at all. I tried to eat some of it, but I just couldn't, so I begged off. So that was our cook. There was a lot of rice and beans that first year.

One woman hitchhiked all the way from New York. She was an older woman, Astar. She followed the Rainbow People festivals, a group of hippies who would get together in different places. They still meet on a yearly basis and exchange pot seeds. They have a big love-in fest. I've never been, but this is what Astar told me. She pitched a small tent over a piece of rope and tacked it down on both sides, so she had a little triangle to crawl into with her bedroll. While hitchhiking, Astar managed to talk a trucker into giving her huge gunnysack bag full of chilies. During the preparation days, she roasted them, stuffed them with cheese, dipped them in an egg batter and made Chili Rellenos. The chilies were so hot we couldn't eat them. Most of the women scraped the cheese out of the peppers, and the breading off the top, and even then the capsicum in the chilies was extremely hot.

ICE CUBES IN THE SWEAT LODGE WATER BUCKET

On the second day of a Sundance I participated in, in South Dakota, during the midday Sundancers' sweat, I told the story of being at Sundance when a young man there was sweet on me. The dancers, including me, were resting between rounds. This young man stood behind the dancers and said, "Well, I've got to go. I've got to go haul water for your sweat."

I answered, "Could you throw a bag of ice cubes in there while you're at it?" He just laughed.

When we got into the lodge, they handed us the water; it was a bucket of water filled with ice cubes. A woman named Ellen was pouring. She let out a yell and demanded to know, "What is this?"

The young man said, "Your girls asked for it."

Ellen was furious, and said, "Who asked for this?"

So, I had to say I did. She just looked at me and she said, "You're not supposed to be talking to anybody." Nobody told me that, so I didn't know, I told her. When she closed the door to the lodge, she used that whole bucket of water on the rocks. Let me tell you, it was hot. We were scorched when we came out of there.

It was hot in the desert where we held the women's ceremony, When they opened the door of the sweat after the second round, somebody said that they were burning up, that it was much hotter dancing in the desert than it was in South Dakota. But I said, "Oh, it's not much different. It can get really hot in South Dakota, too." I stuck my head out the door, looked up at the sky—which was clear—and I said, "Looks like snow and ice to me." Then I stuck my head back in the lodge and everybody laughed.

When we returned to the arbor that afternoon, the clouds rolled in, the sky opened up, and golf-ball sized hail fell. We were all laughing because those who had been in the lodge with me knew what I had said, so we all stood around with our shawls up over our heads. Everybody was covering themselves as best they could because our arbor provided us with very limited shelter. Then, as quickly as it had started, the storm passed. When we continued dancing, we felt incredibly blessed.

THIRTEEN SUNDANCERS

Thirteen Native American women came to Sundance together. When they talked to me on the phone beforehand, every one of them said they'd been to Sundance before. To me that meant that they had pledged to dance and danced for two or four days. But when we all assembled, it became clear that only myself and

141

my daughter, Lushanya, had completed a four-year pledge. The Sundance cycle, once completed, indicates one's commitment to the community. Most of the thirteen women who had supported a Sundance, had stayed for only one day, usually the last day. So, it was in that way that I found myself in the position of having to teach. My expectation was that these women would participate as Sundancers, that we would come together and teach the rest of the community, but suddenly I was in into the position of having to teach everyone there. One woman offered to sing the Sundance songs, but she only knew one or two . She was also into S&M and she wanted to sit at the drum wearing her full leathers. Oh, dear.

The first time I was alone in the lodge with the thirteen Native American women who were going to dance they had a lot to say to me. No sooner was the door closed then they expressed their concern that when they walked across the land and looked up, all they could see were white faces. They were furious, they said. They hated it that there were white women on the land. Why couldn't they go away? We went around the circle and every one of them expressed in no uncertain terms how unhappy they were that there were white women at Sundance. I said, "Well, this is a ceremony of my people and these white women have been invited to provide support. Did you know that it was one of the whitest women here who came several weeks in advance and cut all those branches for the arbor by hand? There was no one else here. There is also a white woman here who came to cook. She drove all the way here from New Mexico in her camper van with no request for help. She's taking care of the kitchen, making sure that people are fed. Did you know that the food that's been provided has been donated by the white women who have been putting money into a jar?"

Their answer was, well, yeah, but they owe it to us. I said, "I understand how you feel. But that attitude is not going to help any of us anymore. It is not going to help our children or our grandchildren or their grandchildren. We have to think of them. I will not ask these women to leave. We need them. We need their voices at the drum. You've come to serve and pray. That's your role here. Theirs is to serve and support. Looking at colour is not going to bring healing." They all started in with the history of colonialism, but I interrupted and added, "Like I said, I understand, but I won't allow that here. This is not the place for that. I'll put a trash can at the end of the road and if you have any gripes or animosity or ill feelings, leave them in the trash can. Then when you leave, the trash can will still be there and you can pick everything back up and take them with you if you like. Then you can speak your voice. But while you're here, this is one of the rules. We work together." They weren't happy.

I had been taught that when you line the women up, you line them up according to the years that they've danced, and if we had two women who had danced exactly the same number of years, then you stand the oldest in front of the younger one. The woman who owned the land, Zelema pledged to dance. She was a medicine woman. Four days before I was to head up to the land, Zelema called me and said, "I didn't get my dress done. I want to dance, but I don't have a dress or a shawl." So, I made her a dress and another woman fringed the shawl. Zelema hadn't prepared any tobacco ties either. Each dancer is asked to bring four hundred and five small bundles of tobacco to offer to the spirits of the tree. These represent the prayers we offer during the ceremony. Several of the women sat up with her one night and helped her make the four hundred and five tobacco ties, one for each of the spirits who watch over the ceremony. I allowed it because I knew it wasn't her people's way and she was new to Sundance. My original expectation was that as a woman who considered herself a healer, she would and should know the importance of these things, but then I realized that I was making a judgment and that I had no right to do that.

When we got to the arbor, I positioned Zelema as the oldest—she was about fifty then. Lushanya, who had already danced eight years in her short life—four years of one day at Sundance, and then four years of two days—and was now beginning her four days, stood next to me. Zelema was furious. She felt that it was disrespectful of me not to acknowledge her as *the* medicine woman at the ceremony. She did not say that to me at the ceremony, she held it in. It was a very powerful dance. At the same time, it was harsh for the women that first year. Very harsh.

But my inner voices were telling me that this place was not where we would continue to Sundance

We had a couple of other fires that needed to be put out. Some of the women were unable to sing in the high falsetto voice of a lot of traditional women. Women were coming to me and saying they were being told that if they didn't sing "right," they couldn't sit at the drum. I said, "No, no, no. You sing in the way that you can. Let it come from your heart."

I called Zelema several times during the four months that followed Sundance, but she never responded. I was baffled, so I wrote a letter, then called and left another message that I'd written a letter. I received a message back that Zelema would not speak to me, and that she was very offended by what I had done to her. It was in that way that we began a dialogue about what happened. I tried to explain what I had been taught about the lineup and that that was the way it was done. She said, "Well, not on my land. I'm the one who loaned you the land that held the ceremony. I should have been honoured as *the* medicine woman."

It became clearer to me that her land was not the place for us to hold the Womyn's Sundance. When spring arrived, we took the arbor down. Another woman had offered the use her land. She had forty acres about fifty miles away. The white woman who had cut all the cedar for us, called me and screamed; she said I'd dishonoured her ancestors, that her ancestors were witches who were burned at the stake. She added that I'd dishonoured her by taking the arbor down because that was *her* arbor. To this day, she is still angry at me. So we rebuilt. This time we built a Ramada that was twelve by eight to shelter our kitchen. The new grounds were in the desert and there was no water, so we hauled water from a nearby town, about fifteen miles away. That's where we danced our second year.

SECOND AND THIRD YEARS OF WOMYN'S SUNDANCE

The second and third years of the Womyn's Sundance were very difficult. I knew I should not—could not—continue Sundancing with Charlene, who had taken over leadership with almost no guidance from a Lakota Elder except for myself in these two short years. There was far too much friction between us and I was not able to assert myself, or my leadership, because the abuse cycle between us was still very much alive. I recognized that it was time for me to follow my own dreams about a Sundance for women, my own dream of spreading the avocado seeds, and to continue to provide women with the opportunity to Sundance at an all-womyn's ceremony. I thought I had found the answer in 1990, at a two-spirit gathering in Winnipeg. I was sure that was where I would go. While I was there, a woman offered land for us to build an arbor. Other women also offered their support and help. And everything began to fall into place.

KEVIN, THE PSYCHIC

Then I went to a party at Heather Bishop's place in Manitoba. There was a man there by the name of Kevin. Heather told me he was a wonderful psychic and that he was so right on about everything. I thought, oh great, another white psychic and a man at that. At some point during the evening, Kevin came up to me and said, "Only thirty dollars for a reading."

Well, I had no money so I said, "I don't want to pay thirty dollars to hear some white man tell me what he thinks my life should be." I had come into the house to use the restroom and as I started up the stairs, he stepped out of the room where he was working, looked at me and said, "You are the reason I'm here." I thought, oh man, what a lie. I bet he says this to everyone. He asked if he could have a few minutes with me. I reminded him that I wasn't one of his clients, and he said, "No, I know you're not." That startled me. I didn't expect him to readily admit that.

So, I followed him into this room and sat down with him at a card table. I looked at the cards on the table and he immediately said, "Oh, ignore the tarot cards. That's just so I can keep my hands busy." Then he asked to see my bracelet and when I gave it to him, he started to tell me about my children and my relationship with every single one of them, with accuracy. I was impressed. He then started talking about where I was in my life with such precision that I was speechless. He said, "I don't know who I should be addressing, you or the dozen people who are standing behind you." He began describing the people he saw behind me. Many of them were my spirit guides. I was shocked that he would know this because I don't talk about that to many people and I'd never met this man before. Kevin didn't know anything about me. I didn't know anybody else at that party and I was thinking, how does he know all this about me?

He told me that I was going to go to a mountain and hike into the valley. He said there's a pool of water there and you're going to drum and meet another spirit guide who's going to take you on a journey.

I said, "I was thinking of moving to Winnipeg."

He said, "There's nothing in Winnipeg like that. I don't see it in Winnipeg. Maybe in New Mexico?"

I was baffled because I was hell bent on going back to Arizona, doing my banking, and moving to Winnipeg. "I don't think so," I said. "My plans are to move to Winnipeg when I get back." He thanked me when we finished and I asked him how much I owed him. But he was true to his word, "Oh, no. I told you, you were the reason I came here. I don't want money from you. I should be giving you money." And he did! He gave me a hundred dollars. I walked out of there stunned. I told Heather what happened and she was stunned too. From that moment, I pondered on where I was going to move.

I found myself back in Arizona living with my daughter Lushanya, doing per diem work and saving every penny I could. I began to talk to some of the Elders I knew. One of them was Ida Amiott. I talked to her about what had transpired and she said to me, "Well, my girl, you have to make a decision. Either don't do the Sundance at all, or go somewhere and lead it by yourself, but you can't continue to be where Charlene is right now." I immediately began to pray about it. I went down to Southeastern Arizona and my friend Carol—who had helped me move—asked me to go with her on a six-week trip. Carol was a performer. She sang and she was a writer. I went with her because I saw it as a perfect opportunity to meet up with women I knew, and women I didn't know, to talk about the Sundance.

BIG CHANGES FOR THE FOURTH YEAR

We travelled to Denver and then to South Dakota, where we stayed at my brother's for about a week. This was interesting because Carol was from a white middle-class family and she'd never been on the reservation. We left the highway up near Wall Drug Store, which is a major highway—I think it's I-90—and cut down to go to Pine Ridge, which is about another hundred and fifty miles south. I asked her if she wanted to get something to eat because it was about seven o'clock and she said, "Oh, no, we can get something along the way."

I laughed. "You don't understand," I told her, "There's nothing on the way."

She didn't get it, "Oh, we'll find something."

But I assured her there was nothing on the way. She kept insisting and I kept telling her, no, there would be nothing. The towns you go through, they don't have fast food restaurants, I explained. "Pine Ridge does not have McDonalds or anything like that."

We ended up getting lost and not arriving at my brother's until midnight. It was a three-hour drive and we got there at midnight, nearly six hours later. We pulled into Pine Ridge and there was a little fast food—Taco John's. I started laughing because it was fairly new and I'd insisted there would be nothing like that. It was closed, of course. When we got to my brother's, he had a bunch of people there. He'd been waiting for us, so as soon as we came into the house, they had a pipe ceremony. My brother's wife had made a cake to honour us being there. So, here we were at two in the morning eating cake and drinking coffee, which was totally foreign to Carol. It was a small trailer. They had cleared out one of the rooms. There was a twin bed and a mattress on the floor. I said, "I'll take the mattress on the floor."

She sat down on the bed and she said, "No, my back is bad. I'll take the mattress on the floor."

I said, "Okay."

Carol opened the closet. She was going to set our bags in there and when she opened the door, there were buffalo robes hanging and a string with dried deer meat on it. She said, "Oh." I told her they were just drying the meat in there. She looked at me, closed the closet door, lay down on the floor, got into her sleeping bag and turned over. I had a little chuckle, got into the bed and pulled the blankets up. When I did that, the blankets lifted up on the side of the bed next to Carol.

Carol shrieked, "Jesus Christ!"

I laughed and said, "Not in this house." I asked her what was the matter and she said she couldn't sleep on the floor because of all the skulls that were staring at her. Turns out my brother had five buffalo skulls under the bed. Carol was in major culture shock. It was really hard for her to be there, but in the end I think it was a good thing.

After our visit there, we went all the way to the East Coast, to Annie Benedetto's house in northern New Jersey. Carol did a performance up there and I lead a sweat. We drove back down by way of Ithaca, New York, down to South Carolina, which is where I had put the lodge up for Susan Riggins. They asked me to come and lead lodge there. Then we went on into Atlanta, Georgia, and back down to Arizona. We had a really wonderful trip and during that time we became friends.

After returning to Arizona, Carol called me one weekend and asked if I wanted to go camping. I was happy to go and we drove to the Coranado mountains in Eastern Arizona. No sooner had we set up camp that we got rained out. Totally rained out. So on Saturday afternoon I said, "You know, this is not fun anymore." We were in the hills just behind her mother's house. We hiked down about two miles to her moms who suggested, "Maybe you should take a drive over to the Chiricahuas mountains." I asked her where that was and she said, "It is a mountain range about eighty miles from here."

So, we got dry and then drove to the Chiricahuas mountains. When I got out of the car, the land took my breath away. We started hiking in the canyon and I had this strong feeling that I had been down that road before. When we got to the bottom there was a pool of water that was filled by a creek, and I knew that this was the place that Kevin had been talking about when I was in Winnipeg. I didn't see a town nearby so I wondered how I could live there After we got back to our car, we took a different road, that headed toward a small town. I wanted to see what the town looked like. As we were driving, we passed an adobe house. It had a big front porch that ran across the whole front of the house. It was an old house and I suddenly had a premonition. I said to Carol, "I'm going to live there."

Carol was surprised, "You're going to what? Did you tell the people that own it that you're going to live there?"

I said, "No, not yet."

Then we drove through the little town called Bisbee, to a café called The Winery. While we waited for our food, I grabbed a newspaper and scanned the "for rent." A three-bedroom house was available for three hundred dollars a month. I went outside, found a public phone and made an appointment for the following day. "Let's just go and see what it looks like," I said to Carol. "She told me where the key is."

Carol agreed and off we went. After we had a look around, I said, "Yup. This'll work." It was not the adobe house; that house came later.

"But you don't even have a job, Beverly," was Carol's stunned answer.

I shrugged and said, "This is where I'm supposed to be. I will get all my stuff out of storage, rent a U-Haul truck, and drive it down from Phoenix."

She said, "You're crazy."

I said, "Yeah, I've been known to do things like this. I need to be near the Chiricahua's and this is as close as I can get right now. This is where I have to be."

Carol came to visit about a week after I had moved in and she said, "I'm going to visit my grandmother. She's in a nursing home. If you'd like to go with me, we can have dinner after." When we got to the nursing home, I got to chatting with the nurse and she asked me to come back the next day for an interview. The next day, I had a job.

Everything just fell into place and I knew I was supposed to be in Bisbee. Bisbee was a really small mining town that at one time had been a booming town of about fifty thousand people. Now it was a ghost town with maybe six thousand inhabitants. There was a hole that had been dug to mine the copper and that hole was so big that every penny in the world could not have filled it up. It was like a big gaping wound on Mother Earth and every time I drove by it, I cringed.

Carol and I became lovers for a short time, and she moved in with me. About six months into that relationship, I wrote Charlene a letter and I asked her if she would please not come to Sundance that year. I said, "Give me a year to be able to put all my energy towards the dance and towards my prayer, without any drama. The last few years have been distracting and I need that space. Give me a chance to heal and then we can move forward." She was furious. And I was bombarded with letters from women who'd gone to the Sundance, telling me that as a Pipe Carrier I should be bigger than that. They thought I should be able to forgive Charlene and not let our past interfere with the ceremony. I actually agreed. I too felt like I should be able to set it all aside, but my fear of the violence was intense.

At Christmas, I went to see Lushanya, who was living in Phoenix and saw Charlene on a regular basis. Waiting for me in her house was a big box, wrapped exquisitely in beautiful pink foil, and tied with pretty big bows. My daughter said, "Charlene left this for you." Inside I found a stuffed rabbit and a letter. Her note said, "I found this rabbit at a thrift store and she was looking for a home and I thought that she would find a home nestled near the warmth of your breast. I know that cuddled next to your body, she will be safe. Are you still surrounding yourself with white women who tell you what you want to hear? You're really screwing your life up. I'm the only one who's ever going to love you and you know that. I wouldn't have had to hit you had you not been unfaithful." The letter went on and on and she kept getting more and more abusive. I thought, wait a minute. The letter had gone from, "I love you, I care about you," to something truly hateful. I set it down and said, "I have to go."

I left and went home to Bisbee. I didn't say anything all the way there. I got in bed and all of a sudden I started shaking, violently shaking. Tremors were coursing throughout my entire body. My teeth were chattering and I was ice cold. And then I started crying. It was hysterical crying. I couldn't seem to stop. Carol got really concerned. I got up to go to the bathroom and

I couldn't even walk, I was shaking so bad. She put me in bed and grabbed a bunch of blankets that she wrapped around me. Then she just held me for about an hour, until I stopped shaking. I bit my tongue. I couldn't stop crying. Before leaving, I said to Lushanya, "I don't want anything from Charlene. If she gives you something to give me, I will not take it. Putting you in the middle perpetuates a pattern of her abuse. You're fifteen. You have no business mediating between her and I. This is my relationship with her." Lushanya was angry with me and wouldn't talk to me. It was a rough time.

THE FIRST EIGHT YEARS OF WOMYN'S SUNDANCE

Within days of knowing I couldn't return to lead the Sundance I'd started with Charlene, out of the blue, an older woman, Gail, who owned a hundred and seventy acres of land just outside Bisbee, called me up and said, "You can have a Sundance on my land, only a half mile outside of town, in the foothills." Even before seeing the land I thought, okay, I'll go there and that's where we will dance. I felt Creator was watching over me, helping to bring hope to so many women's lives. And, I thought, whoever wants to come can come. People started coming to see me. A woman came to see me that I hadn't met before. Her name was Elaine. I introduced her to everybody in the room. Lushanya was sitting in a chair holding a newspaper in front of her face, so I didn't introduce Elaine to Lushanya. I went into the kitchen and I thought, wait a minute, that's wrong, so I walked back out and I said to Elaine, "This is Lushanya. She's my baby girl, my daughter. Right now she's not talking, but she's the most important person in the world to me, so I felt like I needed to introduce you. I apologize for not doing so earlier."

Lushanya just looked at me and didn't say a word. She was refusing to go to Sundance with me. She wanted to dance on the land where I started a Sundance with Charlene, but I said, no, we weren't going there, so she wasn't speaking to me. She was fifteen at the time. She went into her room and then stuck her head out, and said, "Mom, come in here." I went in. She looked at me and said, "Okay, Mom. I'll come to the Sundance with you and I'll

Prepping the sweat fire.

Filling the wood shed.

drum. I'll lead the drum. This isn't worth it. You're my mother and I love you. This kind of bickering isn't worth it for me." I cried and she cried. She came and she was our head drummer.

The Friday before Sundance was to start; several women showed up at my doorstep and said, "We're here to dance." Together, we went out to the grounds. There were no trees, so we made a big rock circle and danced in the circle. We built real quick shade for the drummers and a real quick shade for the dancers. We got a large tent because we didn't have a teepee. We were getting ready to dance!

We held the Sundance there for four years. Each year we drew a few more women. It was hard because we were in the middle of the desert. We had to go somewhere else to find everything we needed—wood to burn, water, and supplies. The only thing that was easy for find were rocks. There were lots of rocks. The second year was better because we knew what to expect, so we were able to plan ahead. The third year, I moved into the little adobe house I saw on my first drive through the Chiricahuas. Carol got a job in Wilcox, and the woman she worked for offered the house to her for rent. Carol called me and said, "I've been offered to rent that adobe house."

I said, "You said yes, of course."

She was uncertain, "Well, I didn't know if you wanted to commute."

I said, "I don't know why, but I need to live there." It was a sweet little house. It was old and a little dark because of the porch that wrapped around the front, but it stayed cool in the summer, which was nice. There was a little creek that ran across the road from us so it wasn't like we were totally without water. I thought it would be a temporary place to stay but we wound up being there for two years. We built a lodge, and talk about scrounging for wood! Someone had put in a new fence and they had pulled up all their old poles. They had laid them on the side of the road, so I took my truck and had someone walk behind it, pick up those posts and throw them into the back. They were cedar posts. When we heated the rocks with them, they smelled wonderful. That was the fourth year that I lead the dance by myself. It got to the point where the people who came to join us were really committed to the dance. There was no drama. The only one to insist on certain rules was me. I insisted that things be done a certain way, the traditional ways that I had been taught, but, other than that, everything was pretty mellow.

Each year the Sundance got bigger and bigger and stronger and stronger. But it was a challenging place. We had monsoons. One time, everything was washed away and we had to start putting everything together all over again. The heat was extreme. You had to wear moccasins out on the sand because it got so hot it would burn your feet. At nighttime, when we were all in the tent, we slept on the ground. We'd wrap our bedrolls in big blue tarps and/or black plastic tarps so that if it rained our beds would stay dry and we wouldn't have to sleep in a wet bed. Tarantulas came through camp, visiting. A tarantula would walk across us while we were resting. To say it was challenging is an understatement. We had to stretch our limits and open our minds to new perspectives. And we had also some challenging people join us, different people with different ways of being.

After those four years in the desert, a Native woman and her non-Native partner came to Sundance. They were buying three hundred and thirty acres in Trinity Forest. They said they wanted us to have the next Sundance there and they were willing to give us forty acres. But it became clear that a tree was not going to grow in that arbor because the soil was so poor. That was not where my next arbor was going to be. While we danced for four years in the Trinity National Forest, it was not destined to be a permanent home for the Womyn's Sundance.

After all our years in the desert and in the forests of California, we moved our arbor to Huntington, Vermont, where we still are today. For the first ten years in Vermont, we held the Sundance at HOWL, a collective of some fifty-plus women from all over the world. HOWL stood for Huntington Open Women's Land: for women only. They are very separatist, so boys over a certain age are not allowed on that land. We danced there, and every year we left the land nicer than it was when we got there. Pam, my wife of many years now, keeps the area mowed. When we started, the field where we held our Sundance was rough terrain and overgrown, but when we left it looked like a golf course.

WOMYN'S SUNDANCE TWENTY-THREE YEARS LATER

Keeping the Sundance going has not been easy, but at the same time, I've never felt more certain that I am doing the right thing. So many women have been helped throughout the years. And we have established the beginnings of an all-Womyn's Sundance for future generations to continue this prayer, it is a safe place for women to come and pray for Mother Earth, for their families and communities, for each other. We just completed our twenty-third year. There are some women who have joined us every single year. When we first started, Leonard Crow Dog heard about our Womyn's Sundance and he did everything except put my picture up in post offices as someone who was doing something bad. In his wife's book, *Lakota Woman*, she talks about the lesbians down in Arizona who held a women's Sundance and how Crow Dog felt about it. He threatened my life. "If I ever see her, I will kill her," is what he said. It really woke me to the fact that the vast majority of Native men are afraid of women's power. They're afraid and because they are afraid, they express themselves in violent ways. I don't understand that. I don't understand why they would be afraid of the very power that gave them birth, which brought them into this world. But I guess the macho brotherhood is stronger than the bonds between a mom and her son? It baffles me.

I was taught that if a woman is on her monthly cycle, she is not allowed to enter the lodge, hold feathers, or be around any sacred objects. I was told it was because during that moon time, we are at the height of our power. Well, when I am at the height of my power, I want other women around. And since I don't menstruate any more, I need that energy. So if someone comes to my lodge and says, "I'm bleeding," I'm happy and they are welcome to enter. Women's power is in being able to give birth, in being able to feed and clothe a child until that child grows into adulthood. Other mammals in the world have their babies and then let them go. But we truly labour when we give birth, and when we give birth it's a gift to our community. It is a gift to our people. We think that child is ours, but that child is going to grow up and be a part of the community that they choose to be a part of. They're going to have other children and those children are going to have more children. In Lakota tradition, it used to be that when a woman had a child she would nurse that child until it was almost five. Then there would be a ceremony and she would give the child to a relative or someone else might take the child. They would keep the child for a year, a year and a half, and then the mother would go back and get her or him. But, throughout her or his childhood, we are taught that we are giving this child to the community. This is played out a lot during ceremonial times. Men aren't able to do that, so they have the piercing during Sundance. I'm told that when the skin tears away from that muscle that it's the equivalent of giving birth. In my experience, only the gay men could stand to give birth. It's worse than anything else I've ever done. The Sundance that the women do is probably really simple compared to the rituals the men follow.

When a child is born, our women used to take that child into the lodge immediately and there were actually some lodges that were built for birthing. They were built taller and they had a different a door, a differently-shaped door in both the front and the back of the lodge. When a child was born, all they would do is bring the flaps down. The rocks would already be cooking, and as soon as the child is born, the hot rocks are brought inside the lodge and all the women there would hold that baby and pray with it as it went around the circle in the dark. This is done to remind us that we were a part of this child's life too, that while mom might have the final say, that child belongs to the community. And that's why we have that child, to replace ourselves and in many cases, to add to the community, so that there are always more people.

And we have so many different kinds of people who come to Sundance and are affected by the ceremony and by the prayer. Some people say, "Well, I can't do anything physical. Then I see them doing things that they didn't believe they could do and they're laughing about it, saying, "Wow! I didn't know I could do this." I've seen women come here and learn carpentry from other women. Once I asked a woman to pick some lettuce, and she pulled it up by its roots. She had never picked lettuce before, so someone then taught her how to harvest the lettuce in a good way. A lot of teaching goes on behind the scenes that we are not always fully aware of until someone points it out. Womyn's Sundance has become a huge spider web that holds women from all over North and Central America.

Sundance has become an entity unto itself. The women don't pierce here because we don't need to. We bleed each month. We already give flesh offerings. The leader and the women who pledge to dance don't eat or drink for the four days of the ceremony. I do, however, allow them a bit of water in the lodge to help them replace what they lose. Taking care of the women and their health is really important to me, and it enables them to open up to creating prayer space. For some people in this society, that's a foreign concept. They don't understand it. They have no idea how to go inside when someone's not telling them what to do. So many people today are not able be authentic if someone's not telling them what to do and how. Women of all colours participate in Sundance, not as dancers, but in other capacities as well. Only Indigenous women Sundance, but there are a lot of non-Native women who come and are healers. We come together so we can share our differences, not take each other's differences, but share them without being afraid of co-opting someone's traditions.

Transgender women are welcome as well. It's been an interesting challenge for some of the women to hear that we would not turn a trans woman away. It is a can of worms that the whole community needs to talk about. There are a lot of issues that are brought up in the community, outside of Sundance. The week of preparation days and the Sundance itself are dedicated to prayer. Afterwards, we are to speak from our hearts and not from our heads. The heart speaks true.

There are inherent meanings to other things as well. We use twelve stones in the sweat lodge during purification, assembled in groups of four. Four is a sacred number in Native ways. Three times four is twelve, and this honours those ancestors. The rocks are our ancestors. They hold great knowledge and the steam from them takes our prayers up to the Creator. Once we go into the arbor, we only use seven rocks. This represents the seven sacred directions and the seven Bands of the Lakota people, the Seven Council Fires. So we honour them as well.

Each one of the Council Fires points to a different direction. I have always been amazed that when I enter a lodge and there are twenty-five rocks, it can be just as hot as when there are twelve or seven rocks. Sometimes seven is hotter. The rocks are a vehicle for Spirit to come through. That's why I use the sacred numbers.

Speaking of numbers, I never wanted more than fifty women, and this past Sundance we had about sixty. I thought, okay, when it reaches a hundred, that's when I'm going to Hawaii. We are dealing with a lot of different personalities and with women who've never been to a Sundance before. We have had to make some modifications to be inclusive. For example, we don't sing all Lakota songs. Some of the songs we sing are from other Tribes. Some of them are in English and from other women who have brought them, simply because it is such an eclectic group of women from many different Tribes and many different regions. They're not all Lakota or all Navaho. That's why the words to the songs are printed up and handed out at Sundance. You wouldn't see that at a South Dakota ceremony. The same songs are sung year after year. At the Womyn's Sundance, each woman who joins us is learning from a different standpoint and usually hasn't been exposed to the teachings that are part of the ceremony. We emphasize the wisdom of Elder, so the older you are, the wiser you are. Older women are always asked first to the meals, and when standing in circle for a long time, the younger women will get older women chairs. We have our own land now, over one hundred and ten acres, held in trust for the next generations. There's so much more. I could write an entire book on Sundance alone.

10.

KUNSI KEYA

KUNSI KEYA. THE TURTLE has always been a symbol for women. A long time ago, when a young woman started menstruating, she was given a turtle shell. That turtle shell became her calendar because the turtles in the northern region have thirteen plates on their backs, thirteen large segments, which are subdivided into twenty-eight small segments all over the shell. A woman could keep track of her moon cycle by looking at the turtle shell and marking it off with a piece of chalk or a little smudge of dirt. It was believed that during the great flood, it was the turtle that rose up and allowed mud to be piled on her back so that the earth could be formed. The turtle carries her home on her back and women in the Lakota tradition also carry their home with them. Lakota woman always have ownership of the home. So, the turtle has always been part of women's medicine, so to speak. When we talked about names for the land where we now are at, I wanted the name to have something to do with the turtle. People suggested many different names but I said, "Well, it really is Grandmother Turtle's land." Everyone agreed, so we settled on Kunsi Keya Tamakoce, which means Grandmother Turtle Lands. Most people just say Kunsi Keya rather than use the longer name. It is a name that embraces all women.

This circle that has been formed by the womyn who have come to Sundance, grows larger with each passing year and has become a family. It provides support and love from afar for so many. I don't know how it happened. I only know it is what I was led to do and I sometimes find myself wondering why. Kunsi Keya, this land. In my wildest dreams I never, ever wanted to own a home. When we bought our home, it was just a small old house in Minnesota. I thought we might live there the rest of our lives. But we were only there for five years. When we came here and we held the Sundance at HOWL, a womyn's land collective in Vermont, I thought it would be nice to have thirteen acres. In reality, there are a hundred and ten acres!

We moved to the land in the Green Mountains of Vermont because we realized that in order to develop it, we had to be there. We put the house in Minnesota on the market and the proceeds from the house went to this land. A large chunk of it went into that first year's payment. Then we had to pay forty-five thousand to have the solar power installed on the property. Then, we had to have water, and a lot money for that had to come out of our pockets, me and my partner Pam's pockets. We had to take out a loan and we're still paying it off. But it was important, so that we could live there. For the first four years we lived in a mobile trailer and hauled water. We didn't have electricity for long time and once we were able to purchase a generator, then we had buy the gas for the generator, which was when gas was three or four dollars a gallon. The generator would run for eight hours on a tank of gas, which was five gallons. So, we lived very frugally when we were in the trailer. We were composting toilets. We had no running shower. And when we needed to bathe, we had to heat water in a pan, take it into the bathroom and pour it over our heads. We did this with our granddaughter and our animals for four years. Fortunately, we had a community that believed in what we were doing.

This hundred and ten acres, these grounds that our Sundance now sits upon, is not ours. It is not mine. It is not Pam's. This house is not ours. It's where we live. It belongs to Kunsi Keya, to Mother Turtle Land. When we die, when Pam and I have passed, this house will not get divided up between our children and grandchildren. What we will leave our children are the objects on the walls—our photographs, our paintings, and other trinkets. Those things are our legacies. But only pitiful amounts of money will be given to them. This land belongs to Kunsi Keya, and will always be here for women to have ceremony. I would prefer that it would be Native women and we'll see how that works out,

Sundance arbor, 2014.

which Native women are going to be able to step up and make that commitment and love the land as much as we do. They need to be committed to taking it over and ensuring it for the next generation. It's harder work than it sounds. It sounds like it's easy. It's not. These one hundred and ten acres are women-owned and women have responsibility for it. Is it closed to men? No. But the positions of power need to be in the hands of women. We need to handle that power and manage it. We need to know how to use chain saws and we need to know how to split wood. We need to know how to tell the difference between hard wood and soft wood, what burns best and what doesn't burn. These are survival skills, many of which have been lost to us. These are some of the things that women learn here, on this land.

One day the arbor that we have here at Kunsi Keya is going to be a fully-grown, living arbor. It will have a full circle of mature trees. It won't have the same arbor structure as we now know it. It will take a long time, and it probably will not happen in my lifetime. But, if we look at the little tree currently in its centre, we can see how much it's grown in just the past four year, five years,. So, I know that the other trees, when they start to grow, will be be pretty phenomenal. I realized when I had my vision, that the trees

Altar in the arbor.

are our life. If all of the trees on this planet were cut down, we would not be able to breathe. If even half of them were cut down, our air quality would suffer dramatically. Trees filter the air so that we can breathe. I look across the world and I see so many places on this planet where trees are mowed down so that people can build. They are chopped down and never replanted. There are some people who are aware of the danger and do replant, but there are many more people who do not. And so, as women at the Womyn's Sundance, we recognized the need to plant trees rather than take them down.

As women, we need to give back to the earth. It gives me a great joy when I hear that a tree has been planted. We planted a small circle of trees, and, by doing so, we are giving back. We do not cut down a new tree every year. In South Dakota, at all the Sundance's, about ten trees are cut down to prepare the arbor. That may not seem like a lot, but if you do that year after year after year, in ten years, you will have cut down a hundred trees. If you go outside right now and count a hundred trees, you will see what a large area they cover. Those trees are cleaning our air. At the Womyn's Sundance, we stress the importance of giving back—giving back to Mother Earth.

I think this is what makes the Womyn's Sundance different from the men's dances. At all of the Sundance's I've been to, after a man has been pierced, he is lead around the circle and everyone cheers and hoops and hollers for him. In this way, he is honoured for having broken free from the thongs in his chest or the skulls on his back. But when a woman gives birth, women are not lead around their community so that the people near her can cheer her and honour her. It's usually only other women who understand the pain she has gone through and what she is given that understand and honour her. So, it is really different. It has been suggested that our tribes, our communities treat women differently than they did two hundred years ago. Long ago, our communities were matriarchal, and women were honoured, their wisdom acknowledged, their fertility considered divine. Sadly, I don't know anybody two hundred years old who I can talk to about this. If I did, I'd be sitting at their feet bombarding them with questions. None of us really know what life was like two hundred years ago, any more than someone will know what our life was like two hundred years from now.

At the Womyn's Sundance we pray for the healing not just of our planet, but of each other and of all the abuses. Traditionally women were honoured as the ones who gave birth, the ones who carried on the male seed. But today women are undervalued everywhere. Everywhere. Even among the Lakota's. Take, for example, the case of Archie and his daughter and son. Josephine was the first-born. She should have been the next in line to pick up his sacred things and carry on that tradition. She'd been taught the traditional ways, but she was bypassed and not even mentioned. Not even mentioned. And the respect and Chief's bonnet and staff were presented to Josephine's younger brother, John. This young woman, who travelled to Europe with her father, who sat next to her father, who watched and learned from her father, was not even acknowledged. And that was not so long ago. That was only about seven years ago. This exemplifies where our people are at, at this time in history. I'm not talking about things that happened way back. Today, even women don't value themselves because they've not been taught to do that. I see it at Sundance. I see women come to Sundance searching for something.

Josephine eventually got married and she had a child. A while back she asked me to come to her house. She lived in California. She apologized to me then. I didn't know why she was apologizing to me. She said, "I'm apologizing because I didn't stand up for you."

I said, "When?" And then I asked her to explain.

She said, "We were at Grampa Crow Dog's. I listened to my father agreeing with him about keeping the lesbian and gay ceremony and I said to my father, 'What would you do if I was lesbian?' He said, 'That's not the case.' She said, 'But you never know. Grandma Beverly has been a part of our family as long as I can remember, so how can you sit there and let them talk that way about her?' My father said to me, 'You don't understand. This is adult talk.' I said, 'You think that I don't understand, but I do, because I have friends in school who are gay.'" She looked at me and added, "He wasn't listening to me. So, I wanted to apologize and tell you that I support you and that I look forward to the time when we can sweat together and I want my son to sweat with you." That was a beautiful affirmation, to hear from this young woman, because it took a lot of courage for her to stand up to her dad that way, to say those things to her dad. I think that Josephine, Jose, is a strong woman and she's going to give any man a run for his money. She's an incredible young woman.

Homophobia is alive and well in many places on the reservation. I think it's better now than it was, say thirty years ago, though. I've talked to people since I was asked to leave the mixed Sundance and they've said there are two-spirit people there this year and I thought, what's happening? This is a good thing. It is finally becoming a place where two-spirit people can go and be safe and I think this is important in Indian country, because two-spirit people are part of our culture. There are so few Indigenous people left that we cannot afford to throw anyone away just because they love someone that we don't think they should love. Who said that you can only love a man or you can only love a woman? It's a gift to love somebody. It's a gift to know how to feel for someone. There are so many people in the world who don't know how to feel, who don't know how to love, who don't have a concept even of what it is to love themselves. So, when you're able to love another human being, why would you want to take that gift away or throw that gift away or belittle that gift in any way?

There's an old saying that says if what you're searching for isn't within, you'll never find it without. I think this is true. I think it's very true. Spirit is something that we have within us. I think Native women, and those of us who carry recent memory of Native blood, are closer to it. We're able to tap into it sooner. The Sundance that I envisioned was a place for women of all colours to come and to dance. At this time, we only women of Native ancestry dance. We set that in place because we recognized that even women with Native ancestry often don't fully understand our traditions or the ceremony. We request that someone who joins us come to Sundance for four years before pledging to Sundance. There's no formal training that takes place during those four years, but just by attending, those who participate learn about the fire, learn about all the things that are required for that one to step into the arbor. It takes that long to simply get a glimpse of the commitment that you make. And even at that, we have had women pledge, dance for only one year and then leave. They didn't quite understand why this commitment would not result in their being a "medicine woman. What they were searching for wasn't within and they weren't able to find it without.

When Native women—who usually find it much easier to access Spirit—don't understand, then those that are of European decent are going to have an even harder time. So, until the time we, as Native women, have a strong core within Sundance, there probably won't be all four directions dancing in the arbor. It may happen in a way that's different than I have envisioned it. We now have women who come to Sundance who are of Asian and Native decent. We have women who come who are of Black and Native decent, those who are of Irish and Native decent. In this way, all four colours are represented. The Hispanic women who come are Spanish and Mestizo. They are still Native. They are of Native decent, whether they are from the Dominican Republic or from Barbados—they are all of Native decent. So, I think it's happening. The women I hear from the most are the women of

European decent. They are the ones who are the furthest away from Spirit and who are trying desperately to reconnect with Spirit. I think it will happen slowly, organically.

I learned a long time ago that when you have a vision, it doesn't mean that things are going to happen the next day. Initially, I thought they would. I don't know what I thought; maybe that we would have a miracle and grown trees would simply appear magically. It took me four years to realize, wait a minute, the trees were full grown in my vision. We planted the trees and the trees are growing. Kunsi Keya is the closest that I've come to seeing the beginnings of the fulfillment of my vision. Only in recent years I have recognized that I may not see the entire arbor made up of fully grown trees. I may never see a time when everyone is in the arbor dancing. But, I had to plant the seed because that's what I do. Those are the little frog seeds. I can't go to the spirit world until I get the frog seeds planted, and I feel it's a privilege and a blessing that I'm able to even see the centre tree stand fifteen feet tall after having first planted it as a little twig. Time is different when you look in those terms. My father once said that even a blade of grass changes right before your eyes. If you watched it through a microscope you would see it changing, and that everything changes, but we don't always see it until it's changed. I see the change in the women who come to Sundance. I see the women come and I see that they are afraid. I see that they are uncertain. I see women who come and have never camped before and the thought of using a port-a-potty, never mind squatting in the bushes and peeing, is like, oh, my god, so primitive. What do they think their ancestors did? Do they think they always had flush toilets? The changes happen.

At Sundance, there is so much symbolism behind everything and it takes years and years to learn themwhat those symbols mean. You hear someone talk about the symbol behind this and the meaning behind that, and by the next year, it's all forgotten. Maybe, you'll remember a part of it, because that's how we are as human beings, but it takes years for those meanings, and those symbols, to become engrained inside of you. It takes years for these ideas to really set in. And then it becomes a way of life. And those ways become something you do automatically.

So, Womyn's Sundance is different. It's different in the way that the values are being taught. And the values being taught are about empowering ourselves to teach our children to move ahead. There are more and more men who are becoming consciously aware of the earth they live on. There are even men who dare to cry alongside a woman when something happens. Those are our allies. Those are the ones that we want to continue with us on this journey of trying to heal the earth.

When people come to Sundance, many times I am asked, "What can I expect?" I say to them, "I can't tell you what your experience will be. I can't even begin to give you a hint, but I can promise you one thing with all my being, and that is that your life will change forever. You'll never be the same after you leave that lodge and leave that Sundance. You will never, ever look at the world the same way."

I've never had someone come to me and say, "You lied to me, Beverly." They've all said, "Boy did my life change." And I have nothing to do with it.

I have no idea why or how this happens. It's all about Spirit, Creator. It has nothing to do with me. I am only the one who knows the steps of the dance.

SUMMER SUNDANCE, 2011

It was very thrilling in 2011 to see so many young women at Sundance. And to see these young women taking care of the little children. To see young teenagers—twelve and thirteen—walking, and holding the hands of a three-year-old boy or a four-year-old girl, taking care of them. Volunteering to sit in someone's camp so the mom could go to the sweat at five in the morning. These were the gifts I saw at Sundance that year. These were the things I was able to witness by not being in the arbor. I was able to see a different picture and it truly felt like an incredible blessing. I hope that other women who come to Sundance get to witness this rather than getting so tied into worrying about whether this colour is in the right direction or not.

This reminds me of a story. Years ago, I was asked to sew the flags for Sundance. On our grounds, we fly the colours of each direction and a rainbow flag. That rainbow flag is to show that we are open to two-spirit people. But this was before Kunsi Keya. I was asked to sew the four directions and a four-directional flag. So, I would sew a flag for each of the four directions and then one flag that had red, yellow, black and white strips. I sewed this flag. It was about two feet of fabric. It was a good size flag. I took it to Sundance, spread it out, and Archie said, "Well, it's nice but the black needs to go here. That's the wrong order." I had to painstakingly take the seams apart, put the black strip where he had wanted, and then sew it all together again by hand because I didn't have a sewing machine. I took it back. By then a man named Matthew King had arrived at the camp. He said, "That's nice, but you have the black in the wrong place. It needs to go here." So I took it apart again, moved the black again, and when it was done, Matthew came. He said, "Ah, you can't fly that flag. It's got the wrong colours in the wrong places." So I had to take it apart and put it together again. Then another man came and said, "That's not the way it's supposed to be." And you know, by the time I was finally finished, the colours on the flag were in exactly the same order I had them in to begin with. I laugh about it now. I think of all the energy I spent taking it apart and sewing it back together again. These men had difficulty making up their minds where the colours were supposed to go, but Spirit knew all along.

In the end, the most important things to me are the women, and my desire to impart even a tiny bit of wisdom to empower them and help them move into their highest potential, to be the best of who they are going to be. I oftentimes tell people, you may do something in the lodge as you're pouring water that goes totally against what I have taught you because Spirit has told you that's how you have to do it, and I'm here to tell you that if you go against what I taught you, you darn well better do it well. But you better do it, no matter what I say. Spirit comes to me all the time and who am I to say that Spirit didn't talk to you? That's kind of who I am. I feel like that's what I was put here for. That's the work that I have to do in this lifetime. It's hard because so many women don't see themselves as worthy. It's because of this darn system we have all lived under that has convinced women they are not worthy. I am convinced that if all the men on this planet were to suddenly die tomorrow, there would be peace on earth. There would be peace between all the countries.

A BUFFALO ROBE HONOURING

Over the years, buffalo skulls have been brought to us at Sundance. They say that when you are honoured with buffalo skulls for your ceremony, it is an acknowledgment that what you're doing is powerful, that the medicine is there. So we have all these buffalo skulls now and that in itself is an honour—to dance with them, with the spirit of those animals there in the arbor with us. When someone is honoured for what they have done in their lifetime or in a certain situation, they're usually honoured with something extraordinary. A buffalo robe is extraordinary. It's something that will keep you warm, keep you sheltered. It can become many things for you. Recently Lushanya said something about someone being gifted with a buffalo robe, about being honoured that way. I never thought that person would be me.

But, at Sundance, in 2011, I was honoured with that buffalo robe and it was the most incredible thing I've ever felt. To have each of the women come up from the different directions and speak to me was a powerful affirmation. It was just incredible. I had goose bumps. When I lay down on that robe and those women picked me up, words can't describe how I felt. When I looked up I saw a sea of faces above me, singing, I was touched. Really, really moved inside. That buffalo robe is a great honour to me—a great, great honour. And then Lushanya told me the story of how she got the robe. She was online and found this woman who had this buffalo robe. Lushanya asked her where the robe had come from. The woman told her that her husband had gotten it for them to be married on, but it had arrived too late. She'd wanted to work with women who'd been sexually or physically or psychologically abused, and when she was given the buffalo robe she envisioned working with women, having the women lay on it who were experiencing this kind of trauma. Her husband was sick with cancer and they had to move to Florida, and she couldn't use the robe anymore. When she gave the robe to my daughter—they negotiated and Lushanya bought it—the woman said, "Tell your mother that she is holding another woman's dreams and her dream was also to empower women." This woman is from Cheyenne River Agency in South Dakota. Cheyenne River Agency is where my grandfather was born. There are so many things about this story that are simply amazing. I hold that robe with tremendous respect and it's an incredible experience to have been gifted with that robe, and to wear it. I was totally surprised. I wish everyone could experience what I experienced at that moment.

PRAYING TO THE FOUR DIRECTIONS

We pray to the four directions, and each direction represents not just one thing but many things. Yes, the sun rises in the east. But what does it bring us? Sun brings us warmth, it bring us life, it enables us to see clearly without having to strain our eyes, it provides all kinds of energy that we don't see—energy that turns our plants green and helps our plants grow. Our plants need the sun's warmth so they reach up and they grow. When I see the sun shine, and I see a plant, I can see the plant's little hands reach up to the sun, growing, "Give me the warmth, give me the warmth." That's really happening but most people don't look at a plant and see that. When I look to the south, I see the thunder. The thunder usually comes up from the south because thunder and lightning are nothing more than warm air meeting cold air. That's what causes thunder and lightening. So you have the warm winds of the south meeting the cold air of the north, causing this huge collision. Some people see that as a bad thing, but I see it as wonderful. It is the creation of energy. How can you create electricity if you don't have those two elements? When you look to the south, you see all the things that come from the south, like corn, for example. Corn isn't a northern crop. Neither are oranges. Oranges give us the vitamin c we need in winter time. There are so many things that grow in the south that are life-giving and life-affirming.

We look at the west and we think of going into nighttime. It's come to be seen as the direction of finality—when you die, you go to the west. But also, in the west is where Grandmother Moon sets. She controls everything on the earth, all the cycles of the earth—the tides, the movements—she controls all of that with her energy. And her energy draws on the gravity of the earth. As women we're not taught that. We're not taught that there's a reason why the moon shows her full face. It's her gravitational pull. It's not something that you can reach out and touch, but it's happening. It's gravity that keeps us on the earth. If we didn't have gravity, we'd all be spinning in space—although some of us are pretty spacey. The north I have been taught is where the ceremonies are sent from. It is also the space in which we rest and regenerate for the next cycle of growth. Its cold forces us to slow down and go within, something this society does not do well. For me, each of the directions symbolize something, and I believe our ancestors were aware of those things. That's why they honoured all four directions, because they knew that we had to have each of those elements to keep us in balance. So, when I honour the directions, when I turn to face each of those directions, these are the things I am thinking about. These are the things that I have been taught to be aware of and while each person is going to see something different when they look at the four directions, it is important to be aware of what the directions symbolize.

I haven't talked about going to the arbor and the procession stopping four times. To begin the ceremony we all walk to the arbor in a procession and place our offerings of tobacco ties to the tree in the arbor's centre. It's pretty much the same thing. You're inviting the ancestors from each direction to come with you, to walk into that arbor with you. I've had people ask me why do we do that? Why do we stop? Why do we not go across the east gate? The east gate is the gate through which the spirits enter during ceremony and it is important not to block that entrance, not to scare them away. Why do we go up four times with the pipe? Because that's the way the Buffalo Calf Pipe Woman gave it to us. She offered it to us four times. Why is the number four sacred? Because the Buffalo Calf Pipe Woman made it sacred by making those four offerings. She waited four days before she came to the community. She spent four days praying to the spirit world. Everything has a reason, an explanation, and it's hard sometimes as you're moving through it to remember that not everybody knows that. There's a lot still to do and at the same time we are trying to teach everyone all the nuances of the traditions, the symbols, and their meanings.

For some of us, our ancestors come from the four directions and so we are honouring ourselves when we honour the directions and the ancestors from those directions. I think that as time goes by, we're all going to become four-direction people at some point in our evolution. There are some people who believe that all of their ancestors only came from one direction. They believe it with all their hearts. But, you know, none of us knows who our great grandmother or our great grandfather slept with, impregnated, or became pregnant by. There are skeletons in everyone's closet and probably it's a good thing if those skeletons stay in the closet. That knowledge—that there are things in my past, in the past of my relatives, that I don't know—keeps me centred and keeps me honest.

THE FOUR HUNDRED AND FIVE SPIRIT STICKS

There are four hundred and five spirit sticks that surround the arbor. I'm told that at one time the chokecherry sticks were dipped in buffalo blood. It was the blood of the buffalo that gave life to the people that are being honoured and the four hundred and five ties each represent the four hundred and five Lakota spirits that watch over the earth and watch over all the big things. The buffalo blood has been replaced with red paint. Very few people have access to a buffalo they can kill. I imagine that on the plains two hundred years ago it was easy to find buffalo blood because it's what they killed to feed their communities. Times have changed, so now we go to Home Depot to buy paint to paint the sticks red. But knowing that the paint, and the sticks, represent the blood of the buffalo changes things. Often, I am asked, well, what are the names of the four hundred and five spirits? I have to say, I don't know. Nobody told me their names. I was only told there were four hundred and five spirits. They look over things and guard the Spirit of the ceremony while we are there. For now, that's what I know.

Prayer ties.

As soon as those sticks are in place, the energy changes in the arbor. The entire place suddenly becomes sacred ground. Not that it wasn't sacred ground when we walked in, but by the time we leave, if you have any hair on your arms, it will be standing up. Why does that happen? I don't know. I don't have an answer for that. I only know that the energy changes. I only know that something sacred takes place. I only know that the ancestors are there. I don't know how many times I've gone out and we've been a few short and I have heard the ancestors say, "What about me? What about me?" Confused and dazed, I'll go over to the drum and I'll say, "We're missing seven," and someone will say, "Oh, that's these seven," and they're stuck somewhere. How does that happen? I don't know. I don't have a clue. These are the mysteries that I can't teach someone. These are the mysteries that will happen for that one person and the mysteries that occur for that person may be different for another, or they may be the same. But no one ever told me that would happen. No one ever told me that I would have the ability or even be anywhere close to being honoured with that kind of dialogue from Spirit. Now

I tell women, these are things that can happen, so be prepared to receive them and be prepared to pass them on. It's a strange phenomenon when you put these knowings in the context of the world we live in. Our ancestors come from another time, a time we are not familiar with.

STEPPING BACK FROM SUNDANCE

The last few years I have stepped back from Sundance, mainly because of my health. In 2011, I chose not to dance in the arbor with the women or to stay with the women, because I am in a lot of pain. The mornings are the worst time for me. Had I been in the teepee, every woman there would have been concerned about me. All their attention would have been drawn to me, "Is Beverly okay? Should we give her some help? Is Beverly hurting because we've done this?" I didn't want that distraction there. The prayers need to be strong, so I opted not to dance. I said to my daughter Lushanya, "I'll come out at noon."

She said, "If you do, once, great. If not, don't worry about it because we know you're here."

Over the last few years, I've watched Lushanya and witnessed her come into her own being, only by discovering and dealing with her own inner struggles and challenges. She doesn't need to be taught, she just needs to be reminded, and she does well. She does very well. I know that should I pass, she will take over. She has learned a lot about ceremony. She has learned the values and she loves this land, so I know that she'll be the one that steps into my place. And she already has. There are many times at Sundance when we'll have a sweat and I will get out there and I'll realize that there's no way I can sit through all four rounds so I'll hand the pipe to her, ask her to facilitate the lodge, and she does a marvellous job. I know she knows what she's doing. And it's the same for the women who've come through training. I've had several women who've done year-long training. They know what they're doing. As I said before, you don't really own it until you give it away. It's time for me to give it away. It doesn't mean I'm going to Hawaii. I think they've put a block on tickets to Hawaii during Sundance week. Ha ha ha!

11.

MY CHILDREN

I HAVE WAITED UNTIL NOW to talk about my relationship with my children because my children, my granddaughter, who I raised, and all of my grandchildren, are more important to me than anyone or anything else in my life. They are my life: Rick, Gary, Gina, Alexx, Lushanya. After a lot of careful thought, I have to say that I haven't always had the best relationship with my children. First of all, I didn't know how to be a mom. When I had my first child, I was very young and I had no one to guide me. My mother wasn't much of a mother to me, so I didn't know anything. The first time I ever took my child to visit a friend, I took one diaper, one t-shirt, and one little blanket and I was going to be gone all day. I simply didn't know that I'd need to change the baby more than once during the day. Also, my first husband Joe's mother was a Native woman from Mexico. She wasn't Spanish. She was Nahuatl and she didn't even speak Spanish. She spoke a totally different language that was interspersed with some Spanish, so it was really hard to understand her and she spoke no English. She had my husband when she was sixty-three, so she was quite elderly. When my son Rick was born, she had all these ideas about parenting that were completely foreign to me. One of the most comical was something she did for me when I came home from the hospital. I came home from the hospital and my son was premature so when I came home from the hospital I had to leave him there. He was there for three weeks before I could take him home.

The first couple of days I was home on my own, I didn't have much of an appetite. One day my mother-in-law went out—she used to walk everywhere—and when she came back, she had a shopping bag with a chicken's head sticking out of the bag. A live chicken, a big white, live chicken. I said, "Oh, how cute." Chickens and I ... I love chickens. She let the chicken out in the kitchen. I was petting it and I thought, oh, how nice, we're going to have chickens now. We're going to have fresh eggs. Then I went to take a nap and when I woke up, she told me that dinner was ready. She had made homemade tortillas and there were beans, chicken and rice. I ate a piece of chicken and it was really good, so I had another piece. Then I took my plate with the bones from the chicken over to the trash can and when I opened it, I saw that it was full of white feathers. I drew in my breath, and she said, "Well, you liked the chicken. You ate it. You ate two pieces." I was like, oh my god. But in their tradition when someone has given birth, they are not allowed to eat any frozen or old meat. It has to be fresh-killed that day, so that's why she went and got the chicken for me. After that, every couple of days she'd get another chicken and she'd kill that chicken for me. Thank goodness it wasn't a cow.

Then when Rick came home, my mother-in-law didn't want anyone to come visit. Nobody could visit, she said, for a whole month after the baby was home. She kept talking about the "evil eye." I didn't have a clue what the evil eye was. When someone came to visit, she would run into the bedroom, break an egg, and then place it underneath the baby's crib. My husband translated. She said that when strangers visited and a baby was very young, they might covet your child and they might try to take your child's spirit. That's why she broke an egg and put it under the baby's crib. It was a ritual to protect my son. She also didn't believe in bathing him. She would wipe him with a small wash cloth, but would not immerse him in water. She also believed in keeping the baby really warm, so she'd put two or three t-shirts on him. I didn't know anything about taking care of a baby. So, I thought that's what you did with babies. I had no idea how to parent, so she did a lot of the parenting.

When I had my second son, Gary, I knew a little more, but still not a lot, so I kind of acquired parenting skills on the fly so to speak. Even though each of my children, with the exception of my second and third, were about two years apart, it felt like I was barely getting the hang of being a parent and I'd be pregnant and having another one. I did the best I could but I don't know that what I did was best for the child. My mother had been very critical, so I tried to make my children perfect. And, of course, they weren't. They never will be. I know I was stricter with them than I needed to be. After having Gina and Alexx, I decided I wasn't going to spank them anymore. Hitting my children didn't work. It frustrated me and it probably frustrated the kids too, so I stopped. Because of that, Lushanya was the only one of my children who never got spanked. Instead, I would look at her and I'd point my finger, wag it and say, "Don't misbehave. You are going to get a beating. Don't make me beat you." And she'd stop.

That backfired on me though when she was about three. I'd invited a bunch of neighbours over. I'd just moved. I was new to the neighbourhood and I had a Tupperware party. It was a plastic container craze during the sixties that had women hosting parties for their friends and neighbours to sell them the tupperware. I went around the neighbourhood and left invitations in everybody's door. I had about eight women show up that I didn't know that I had only seen in passing. I'd put out a big bowl of sour cream dip with some flavouring in it, and some potato chips. Lushanya loved sour cream. She was sitting on the floor by the coffee table, dipping chips as fast as her little hands could go and stuffing her face. Finally, it was time for the Tupperware saleswoman to give her presentation, so I went to Lushanya and I said, "Come on. It's time to go to bed. Tell everyone good night." I washed her face and hands. She was whimpering. She didn't want to leave those chips.

She shared a room with her sister Gina, just off the living room. I tucked her into bed next to Gina and kissed her good night. As I walked away, I could hear her whimpering louder and louder. I sat down and the woman started talking. In the background the whimpering got even louder and soon turned into a wail. Pretty soon she was screaming like someone was beating her in there. I opened the door and I said, "Lushanya, what is the matter with you?"

She screamed at the top of her lungs, "Don't beat me!"

I froze and the whole room went deadly quiet. I said, "Lushanya Andrea, if you do not lie down and go to sleep at this moment, I'm going to be forced to show you what a beating is."

She said, "Okay, okay," then lay down and went right to sleep.

I turned around and every eye in the room was glaring at me. I said to them, "Oh, no. I've never even spanked her." They all seemed very skeptical, as if, all at the same time, they were thinking, yeah, yeah, right.

I found parenting hard. I had no idea how to parent the boys. Taking them to the sweat, I depended largely on the men at the lodge to give them some direction, but it wasn't forthcoming. The men talked a good talk, but when it came to interacting with the children, they virtually didn't. They didn't give them any beneficial advice or guidance. Except one time that I recall. When we were at Point Conception, little Gary was sitting by the creek and he had pulled a snail out of its shell. One of the men saw him do it. He went over to Gary with a paper plate and he put the snail on the plate, then said, "Gary, you're such a good hunter. I'm so proud of you. Let's take it back over here to the fire so we can honour the life of the snail." He called a few guys over. They all circled around the fire, passed tobacco, and he talked about how when you take an animal's life you have to honour it. They each offered a prayer and they praised Gary for being so brave to kill this snail. They said, "When you kill something, you have to eat it. Unfortunately, this snail is so tiny that it's not going to be enough to feed all of us, but we will stand here and we will honour you while you eat it." Gary's eyes got as big as plates. You could see his lip begin to quiver and he looked scared. He looked at me. I was across the way in the kitchen. I turned and walked the other way because he was looking at me for help. The men put the snail in the frying pan over the fire, and of course it disintegrated. They said, "Oh, Gary, I guess it was too hot. It burned up. Well, you'll have to catch another one." To this day, Gary won't even kill a bug.

When I came out as two-spirit to my children, Rick was twenty, Gary was seventeen, Gina was sixteen, Alexx was twelve, and Lushanya was eleven. I sat them all down and placed them in a talking circle. I told them that I was in love with a woman and that I had loved women most of my life. That didn't mean I loved them any less. I still was their mom, but I wasn't going to be married to a man, and more than likely it would be a woman that I would be spending my life with. They were rather quiet. They didn't have a really big response, nor did I expect that they would, but as the years went by, they would lash out in anger at different times and I understood that was their process. The ones who were the angriest were my daughter, Gina, and my son, Gary. Those two expressed the most anger at my being lesbian because it impacted their social lives and their friends. It made sense because of their ages at the time. I did what I could to help them through their anger. Before friends came over, Lushanya, my youngest, would go through my book case and turn all my books around. She would turn around any book that had "lesbian" or "gay" in the title so the books were not visible.

Later, I worked for the AIDS project in Bisbee, Arizona, for the County Health Department, and I used to get a lot of information about AIDS—this was in the eighties. I would leave the information on the coffee table with a basket full of condoms and lubricants and when Lushanya's friends came over, everything in the basket would disappear. When I asked her about it, she said she would explain to her friends that her mother worked for the health department as an AIDS educator, and the magazines and condoms would disappear. This was early on in the days of AIDS awareness and it was good that her friends were interested.

It was difficult being someone who walks the path that I do because oftentimes someone would call and ask that I bring the pipe, or that I come and do a ceremony for them. It would mean that I had to miss going to one of my children's school performances or to one of their softball games or spending time with them. Maybe we'd made plans to go the zoo and I would have to switch those plans sometimes at the last minute. I think that was the hardest part of my life's work, having to juggle between being a parent and doing the work that I was called to do. There were times when I first began Sundancing in California, that I would get a phone call and be told, "We need all the dancers to come. Such-and-such a person is sick and we're going to have a sweat. We need you to come, bring your pipes and come." I would have to load up the kids and go. That had to be hard for them. It was hard for me, so it had to be hard for them.

Today, they've pretty much accepted that's who I am and that's what I do. They have never hesitated to volunteer me to their teachers to come and talk about Native people. There were many, many times when we had out-and-out verbal confrontations with teachers because my boys all had long hair. That's one thing my boys hated for a time. People would look in the back seat of my car and say, "Oh, you have five beautiful daughters." They all had thick, black hair down to their waists. The boys would say, "We're not girls. We're boys." They would get in trouble at school. We had one principal who used to say, "I see your son running across the field and I think, there goes Chief."

I said, "His name isn't Chief, his name is Gary, and he's not a chief."

He said, "All that long hair, he looks like he could be a Chief."

He didn't get it how offensive that was. My son had waist-length hair and he wanted to play football. They wouldn't let him play football with his long hair. He had to cut it. Of course, we fought that and we lost. It must have been difficult for my children growing up with a mother who was hell-bent on making sure they stayed close to traditions and to understanding those traditions.

My girls, on the other hand, were the ones who would raise their hand in class and say, "Columbus didn't discover America. He landed off of some island. He wasn't here in the United States. And, by the way, how do you 'discover' millions and millions of people?" They asked the hard questions and got into trouble, for getting "off topic," they were told. They questioned what the history books said. And they got into trouble for it.

As time has gone on, the only one who has stayed very close to our traditional ways has been my youngest, Lushanya. She began Sundancing by my side when she was three and has stayed close in that way all her life. This is her chosen way of prayer and following, it's her spiritual path. My daughter, Gina, is aware of what her traditions are and will call me from time to time and tell me she's gone to a sweat and what happened these. She may come to these ways one day. They all may. One of my sons, Rick, who has been incarcerated several times, will write to me and ask me to send him sweetgrass or cedar so that he can pray while he's in jail. He'll complain to me about the people who are coming in to run sweats in the prison he's in. However, he gets irritated when I remind him that when he's not in jail, that there are sweat lodges that he can go to. I don't know whether he does or not, but his daughter recently had a little boy who's now a year old. My granddaughter, Rick's daughter, has come to Sundance at Kunsi Keya and she has put out a call and asked people to send her the words to the songs, to send her a CD with the songs so she doesn't forget them, so she can teach my great-grandson. So, I know that there is still a strong connection for all of them to our traditions and ways, even though it may be indirect. And, I never know when the phone is going to ring and it'll be, "Mom, I want to get some sweet grass, I need to get some sage, I'm almost out of cedar. Mom, how do you sing this song? Mom, how do you say this word in Lakota?" There's still that awareness.

Lushanya, 2008.

Lushanya has, however, definitely stepped into my footsteps and is carrying it beyond anything that I could ever do. She's bright and intense in her learning and she wants to learn. She's

Gina, Takoda, Allysyn and Jordan, 2011.

also an individual thinker—constantly questioning. Gina is very independent, and did not marry until she was thirty. When I broke up with my first lover, she joined the Mormon Church and began sending me all kinds of literature. When I didn't respond to any of it, she stopped sending it. But then when she got married, when she was thirty, she was upset because one of my ex-lovers was going to come to the wedding and she didn't want everybody to know that I was a lesbian. She now has three beautiful daughters. She is now married to a Maidu man from California. She has worked as a firefighter. She chose to actively fight fires and was injured on the job, and is currently in medical retirement from the fire department. She's forty. She and I have a close relationship also. We talk frequently. I'm very proud of her and I love her deeply. I don't get to see her as much as I would like, but one of her daughters came spent a couple of weeks with me last summer, which was really a delight.

My youngest son, Alexx, and I are close also. Alexx had a doll when he was three and it only had one leg. He called it Javier.

Everywhere he went, Javier went with him. Until he was six or seven, Javier sat on his bed. I don't know what happened to Javier. He somehow latched onto this doll and decided it was his to take care of and keep. I always thought that this was very telling about the sensitivity of this huge man, that he would have this gentleness for a doll that only had one leg. My oldest son, Rick, is in Arizona. He and I talk from time to time. He tends not to contact me unless he's been sober for a few weeks. He has a substance abuse issue and when he's not doing well in that department, he avoids me. For the past few years he has maintained his sobriety, I am very proud of him for his choice to do that. So, I have a different relationship with each one of my children. They're the ones that I always pray for as soon as I go into the lodge. I pray for their well-being and to keep their minds clear and help them walk on whatever path it is that they choose.

Beverly and Gary, 2015.

Gary is my second son. He has always been hyper and I guess some people would have diagnosed him with what they now call ADHD. As a young boy, he was always the adventurous one. He was the one who would catch baby rattlesnakes and lizards and

Beverly and sons Rick (left), Alexx (right), and grandson Dalton, 2005.

bring them in the house inside a jar. He was known to run into a wall, hit it head first, and get up and laugh. He was a rough and tumble type of child. When he was about fifteen or sixteen, some of his behaviours began to get disturbing and difficult for all of us. He ran away from home six weeks before I was supposed to graduate from school. A social worker was called. He was staying at a friend's house and the social worker said, "He just needs you to be home, so my recommendation is that you quit school and provide him with what he needs—a mom to be home."

I said, "In six weeks I'll do that, but right now I can't."

The social worker all but called me an unfit mother. I said, "Gary has a home. He is loved. His needs are met. If he wants cookies and milk, I always have milk in the refrigerator and boxes of graham crackers. I'm not going to be able to be a stay-at-home mom for the next six weeks. Our lifestyle is very different. Those are things that happen on TV. They don't happen in everyday life." So, Gary did come home, but he was always pushing the envelope. He would terrorize his younger sisters and brother. He would do things that he knew he'd been asked not to do. He was a challenging child. All the same, I loved him deeply. Each child is different.

I miss my children who aren't close by. I know that I haven't always been a model parent and my mothering hasn't always fit the "ideal" mother mold. A lot of the things that have happened in my life have been traumatic. My behaviour showed it. My behaviour showed it a lot. I could be really mean. When I got angry—I was afraid of getting angry because I would totally explode—I could be verbally abusive. I didn't like that about me. I didn't like those behaviours. When I finally got into therapy and going to the lodge, I found that in the lodge with women, I could talk about those feelings. I was surprised to find that in talking with ten women in the lodge, eight of them would own up to having been abused and to having similar conflicting feelings. I found that a number of Native women didn't talk about what had happened to them, were very ashamed of the abuse, and didn't know how to talk to their children about it, how to warn them. That was me, too. I told my daughters that if any stranger ever approached them or did anything to them, to let me know immediately. I also warned them about grandfathers, I warned them about uncles, I warned them about friends, but I had never warned them about a brother. It was a brother that molested my children. Three years after my son Rick was molested by Teresa and Chemo, he raped my youngest daughter.

Each time that I step into the arbor, a large part of my prayer is for those women and children and little boys—not just little girls, but little boys—who are forced to endure uncomfortable touches and brutal acts that their bodies are not prepared for, their psyches are not prepared for, that their emotions and their spirit are not prepared for. Their bodies are still the bodies of babies. They're still children. I went through a period of feeling anger. I went through a period when I couldn't even go to a park and see a brother or a father playing with their child without thinking, is that jerk going to hurt that little girl? Is he going to touch her in an unwelcome way? I'm glad I moved through that because there would otherwise be a lot of dead men right now. But that was the rage I felt. It came up at me.

When I stepped into the arbor, those were the people I prayed for. I pray for the women in Africa who go to get water, and are raped and beaten, as they leave the confines of a secure area with the other women. The women who are dragged out of their homes, beaten and raped and have to watch their five-year-old daughters be raped, gang-raped, by soldiers. Misogyny against women is a global problem. When I go in that lodge and the door closes and I'm there in the dark, we're all the same. When I pray, I pray for all these women and children and when I do so, I pray for myself, pray to heal those wounds from the past. The pain and the discomfort were horrible. It was terrible. I wouldn't want anyone to have to go through what I went through growing up, what my kids went through, what my granddaughter went through at the hands of her own father. But am I going to let it control my life and ruin my life? I refuse to do that. I have to turn it around somehow, to help other women, to help other young girls and boys.

I'm very proud of the fact that I gave birth to my five children, that they are healthy, that none of them are living on the street. They've all managed to support themselves and take care of themselves. They have the ability to see things from their own perspective and to voice opinions whether I agree with them or disagree with them. I feel that as a parent, my job is pretty much done. I can't affect anything that they do from this point on. Some parents feel, well; I need to be there for my child, right or wrong, throughout their whole life. I don't disagree with that, but I believe that at some point, your children are going to make their own decisions and they're going to follow their own path. I don't have to agree or disagree, and if it's something that's a conflict for me—like with my one son Rick, who used drugs, well, he knows that I have a pipe in my house. He would not come here drunk, nor would he come here under the influence. He respects that. All my children do.

MY RELATIONSHIP WITH PAM—MY LIFE, MY WIFE

When I first met Pam, we were just friends. She was in a relationship. We hit it off, had lots of laughs, and she came to Sundance one year. I don't remember much about Pam being there because it was one of those years when I had struggles with Charlene. Pam and I continued to connect through the years. One of my most vivid recollections of Pam was at Woman Gathering, a spiritual festival for women, mostly non-Native women. My blood pressure had gone up extremely high and they had a physician's assistant in the healing center. It was a healing center where I'd had a massage, reiki, and some acupuncture, but my blood pressure wouldn't go down. So, I was sent over to the emergency room. They told me I needed to see my doctor and come back, and my blood pressure went up again.

A few nights later, I went to a concert they were having. I was walking in and all of a sudden I sat down and it felt like the floor was coming up to meet me. I knew I had to get out of there, so I excused myself. My partner at the time, Carol, was in charge of the lights so she stayed there. I got outside on the lawn and all of a sudden I was on my knees. Pam happened to drive by. She was in a golf cart. She radioed up to the wellness center and told them she was bringing me. My blood pressure was dangerously high again. The physician's assistant said, get her to emergency. They were fearful I was going to have a stroke. She put me in a car and then Pam radioed her partner, Paulette and she said, "I'm taking Beverly to the emergency room. Paulette told Carol and Carol got someone to take her place. Then she and Paulette met us on the road. They jumped in the back seat. We were driving and Paulette said, "I hope you're going to let us get you a wheelchair when we get to the emergency room."

I said, "Oh, Paulette, there'll come a day when I may need that. Today is not the day." But when we arrived, I got out of the car and all of a sudden I felt dizzy. I had pushed the button on my lock and closed the door, so I leaned against the car with my hand up and shut the door on my thumb. My thumb was stuck in the door while everyone was getting out the car and locking their doors. I couldn't move. I was very calm, "Could somebody please unlock the door?"

When they saw that I was stuck, Carol screaming, Pam started panicking, trying to get her keys out of her bag. She'd dropped them in this big old backpack she carried everywhere and she couldn't find them. All I could see through the glass was Pam's face. She was as white as a ghost. And her eyes, those big blue eyes were huge, and she looked totally stressed. She finally found the keys and got the door unlocked and I pulled my finger out. I was holding it really tight and sucking on it, trying to get the pain to go away. We walked into the emergency room and the woman started taking all this information and she said, "How did you hurt your finger?"

I said, "I'm not here because I hurt my finger, I'm here because my blood pressure is too high." I received medication and after about an hour my blood pressure came down. They said, "You need to see a doctor, regularly." They admonished me about it. I came out and Pam and Carol were sitting in the waiting room watching TV. When I motioned to them to let them know I was done, I happened to turn my head and noticed there was a camera, and a monitor. I thought I saw Paulette walking away from a car. I took a closer look, and realized that it was our car. I said to the woman behind the counter, "How long has that been on?"

She said, "It's always on."

I said, "So, you saw me get my finger caught in the car door on camera?"

She said, "Yeah, we wondered what was happening. You guys looked like the Keystone Cops out there."

I think the reason I remember this incident so well is because not so long afterwards, Pam told me she had broken up with Paulette. Then Pam told me she was in love with me. I said, "What about Paulette?" They'd been together about sixteen years.

She said, "Well, it's been over for about five years, even though we've continued to live together."

I said, "That would have to end before I'd be willing to engage in any kind of relationship with you." It was only because of the healing that I had done, the boundaries I had set for myself, that I was able to set boundaries with Pam and to express what I was feeling at the time, without chasing her away for good. To this day, I'm glad for that.

I chose to remain single for two-and-a-half years before becoming involved with Pam, and during that time, I travelled all over the United States. I refused to get involved with someone who had not done their own work, who was not emotionally and spiritually healthy. I had enough garbage of my own to carry without dealing with someone else's. But Pam had done a lot of work. She always had a really good way of relating to people and she's always known herself pretty well. As wonderful as Pam is, though, there are things about her that drive me crazy. She's not a housekeeper. She takes on far too many things and then sometimes doesn't get any of them done. She can be really spacey sometimes. But these are things that I think come with the territory of being an only child. She was an only child. It's amazing because at her mother's house you could eat off the floors that house is so clean. Pam is the opposite. If I didn't remind her the floor needed to be swept, she would see the broom, look at the floor, and keep on walking. But these are benign issues. It's just a difference in how she was raised versus how I was raised. We are able to talk about it and that's the important thing.

Pam has her own spiritual practice. She is Wiccan. She did, and does, her own rituals. She has her own holidays and I support those for her. I will go with her to some of her rituals, but they are not mine and we both know that. Pam knows I do this out of respect for her. I think that coming to the lodge and Sundance has affected Pam's life profoundly. She finds no conflict with what she does and what we do, so she's always been there. I think she does far too much, but she won't slow down. As I've slowly healed, I've learned that love is more than that tickly feeling in your stomach and your sexual organs, and that love is not something you fall into. You don't meet someone and fall in love. It's something you grow into, if you want it to last. And everybody has a different idea of what it means for love to last. Some people are what they

Beverly and Pam, Pride Celebration, Burlington, Vermont, 2007.

call serial monogamists—they get together with someone for ten years and then with someone else for ten years and then with someone else for ten years. That's far too much work for me.

There are times when we have a disagreement and Pam will be the one to say, why don't you bring your pipe out and let's sit down and work on it? I appreciate that about her. If I wasn't on the path that I'm on, I don't know that she and I would be together. Ceremony has impacted all the close relationships in my life. I feel like it's made me a much happier person. Not perfect, but I'm not striving for perfection. Ceremony, and Pam, have been a really good part of my life for a long, long time.

OUR HOPE FOR COMMUNAL LIVING AT KUNSI KEYA

Here on Kunsi Keya, on this land, our goal, mine and Pam's, is to create community. We would like to see people move here and live on the land. That's a difficult thing to do because living here would mean being a part of community and not many people understand what that means. It doesn't mean just coming together once a week for a meal and socializing. It means you get a load of wood, and we get a load of wood, and we come and help you stack yours, and you come and help us stack ours. If there's a snow storm and you're getting low on wood, and we have more wood, you come to our house and we fix a meal together. We are snowed in together. Lushanya and her partner, Kim, live here and oftentimes they will bring something over for mending. Or Kim will come over and ask how I'm feeling that day. I'll tell her I'm feeling really tired, and I'm lying down. The she'll say she'll take care of feeding the dogs, or if she sees that Pam is busy, she'll go out and feed the horses. If I see it's really dry and Kim and Lushanya haven't had time to water their plants, I'll go and water their plants. You see what needs to be done and, where you can, you help.

The town we live near, Huntington, has about twenty-five hundred people and Pam is on the cemetery committee. She's a Justice of the Peace and she's the town dog catcher. I was sitting on the planning commission. The politics were troublesome, so I said, I'm not going to do this and I resigned. But, I'm still pretty active. When they have voting, I go down to vote. I sometimes go with Pam to help count the ballots. We take food to people who are ill. We're on the list to give rides to someone if they have doctor's appointments and they need a ride. We're very involved in the community, and everybody knows us. We try to shop locally. We sometimes go on a kick—when we can afford it—and we get all fresh, raw milk from the dairy. We only buy our maple syrup from Mr. Taff down the hill because he taps some of the trees up here. We do exchanges with J.B. because he has bees and he brings us honey all the time. We take care of each other's animals. One of the women who live across the road and down a bit went away for a week and said, "I was going to come out and see you. We're going away tonight and I was wondering if you could go up to our garden. We have some tomatoes that are ready to ripen, some cucumbers and some basil. Help yourself. I don't want to ruin any of the yields, so just go take it." And so we did. Other friends who live down the hill have chickens, so they'll go away and ask us if we can feed the chickens and the horse and the rabbit for them. They'll say, "We're getting about seven eggs a day. Any eggs you find, just take."

That's what we do. We all have what we need in that way. It helps all of us. In the community itself, we know the owner of the general store, we know the work crew, we know a lot of the people who are prominent in the community. We help put together food baskets at holidays. Sometimes we'll get a phone call from someone who'll ask us to do a wellness check on a person they haven't heard from for a few days and we'll just drive over to check on them and make sure they're okay. We're very much a part of the community in this way. We go to as many barbeques as we can, and as many fundraisers. There's a fundraising spaghetti dinner where all the men cook and all the money raised at the dinner goes to the fire department. There's another one for the Boy Scouts. We probably spend more on those fundraisers than we would normally spend on a meal for just the two of us, but the proceeds go to a good cause. We're not just helping us, we're helping others, and we're helping our community.

This is very important for Pam and I because we want to build a community here at Kunsi Keya and we want to see other people come here and live on the land. This can be complicated because if you get people who've never lived in this environment before, they could burn themselves to death in a trailer trying to get their wood stove hot enough. If it's getting to be cool in the house, it would never dawn on them, to put on a sweater. They think they should be able to run around inside their house naked in the middle of winter. Living on this mountain can be tricky. We feel like the first four years we lived here, when we struggled so hard, it was the mountain's way of giving us experience. It seemed like the mountain was saying, this is the way you need to live. This is the way you live in harmony with me because this is my land. This land is not mine and/or Pam's land. We pay taxes to be here, but it's not our land. It belongs to the community. It's a very interesting position to find ourselves in. On some levels you need what the white world has to offer you, but you want to be in a world that has a different set of values. It's often a struggle, but one of the best struggles I've been involved with for my entire life.

IN THE SPIRIT OF GIVING

When we first moved here, I didn't know what the Christmas holiday was going to be like during the winter and what we were going to have to see us through. Pam was working for the co-op at eight dollars an hour. She'd come from a job where she'd been making about eighty thousand dollars a year, so that was a big change. We still had the mortgage on the house in Minnesota because it hadn't sold, plus our moving expenses to Kunsi Keya, so it was pretty tight. Our granddaughter, Aris, was living with us, and we wanted to get her something for the holiday, so I went down to the thrift store and signed up for a basket. When I did that, an older woman named Fran was sitting there. She had glasses on but one eye was covered with electrical tape. I didn't know if that was because her glasses were broken. She asked for my phone number but we didn't have a phone yet. Fran said, "Well come back, give me your phone number, and I need your granddaughter's social security number. Oh, she's going to be thirteen," she said. "We don't usually give gifts for kids over twelve."

I said, "That's okay. She's beyond the stage of needing toys or anything like that."

She said, "If she were to get something, what would she want?"

I said, "You know, knowing my granddaughter, what she would ask for right now is a warm coat. The coat we got her that we thought it was going to be warm enough probably isn't going to

Beverly and granddaughter, Aris, Minneapolis Pride Parade, 2001.

be." She told me that she would see what she could do and asked what size she wore.

The next week I went back to the thrift store to bring them the information they had asked for. Fran was there and she said, "Oh, I'm so glad you came back. She reached underneath the counter and she pulled out a coat. It was fake fur lined, with a hood, and it was a cute coat. She said, "I bought this. I wore it once and never worn it again. I don't know if the style's too old for her or if she'll like it or if it'll fit. If it doesn't, just bring it back to the store and we'll put it out and sell it. But if she can use it, it's hers." So, I brought it home and I thought, oh, Aris isn't going to like this. But you know what? She loved that coat. She wore it until she couldn't button it any more.

At Christmas time we had to go back to Minnesota for the closing on the sale of our house, so we left Aris with our friend, Char, because we didn't want Aris to miss any school. We had to pick up a food basket. Our friend went to pick it up for us and when we got back, she'd already put all the groceries away. She and Aris decorated our little trailer with a tiny fake tree and they put lights on it that ran by battery, because we didn't have any electricity. On Christmas morning, we had a few gifts under the tiny tree for Aris. She opened them and we sat around munching on chocolate cookies. We were in our PJs—matching PJs. We'd opened the boxes with the PJs on Christmas Eve. The next morning, when we were sitting around our tiny tree in our matching pjs, we discovered a huge bag full of gifts. I said, "Are those Char's?"

Pam said, "Maybe she bought them for her grandkids and left them here by accident." So, we set them aside.

About a week later, Char came, and I said, "Char, we've been hanging on to your gifts."

She said, "Those aren't mine. Those are the ones they gave me when I went down to get your food."

I looked at the tag on the bag. It had Aris' name on it. There were gift cards to book stores and gift cards to record stores and CDs. There was a little CD player. There were things for her hair. There were socks. There was a brand new, warm winter coat—an expensive winter coat—and a receipt in case it didn't fit and had to be exchanged at Sears. I was so touched and moved by that.

The next year I got a phone call from Fran. She said, "We're having a registration for Christmas turkeys for this year and I just wanted to make sure that you knew when the deadline was."

I wrote to her and I said, "Last year was our first year here and we had a really hard time. I was so grateful for the help you gave us, for the gifts you gave to my granddaughter. This year, I'm working and my partner's working and we really don't have a need for a Christmas basket. I prefer that it go to someone who's in a needier place than we are right now. And this year, we're helping a family. We're helping a woman from Somalia who has four little children."

So, the cycle continues. You ask for what you need and then you pass it on. From that time onward, Fran and I established a friendship. I haven't heard from her for a while and I'm concerned because she is elderly. She was the nicest person and her love and caring is one of the things that endeared me to living here in Vermont. Her caring reminded me of the Native communities I grew up in. I have mentioned before that I learned from my father that what you put out comes back to you. So I try to put out there and it always comes back to me. When my father died I couldn't afford anything for a giveaway, so I gave away all my bracelets. I had about thirty of them. Now I have about thirty more because people have given them back to me. Not the same ones, but they've all come back. Life is beautiful and precious. And it always will be.

12.

OUR ROLE AS WOMEN TODAY

WHEN MY TEACHER, Archie Fire, passed, I went to his funeral in South Dakota and his daughter Josephine kept me close to the family. Archie had a son in Europe. The son and his mother were there at the funeral. Archie's wife, Sandy, and the rest of Archie's children embraced this young man because he was their half-brother. There were other women that were there from Germany. One of the women was talking about having gone to sweat lodges in Germany. She said that Archie had run them and they were wonderful experiences. But when she went to the lodge in South Dakota, she added, the spirits were there and she said she wondered if it's because in European countries people have stepped away or basically isolated themselves from our traditions, our earth-based traditions. That's what she called them—earth-based traditions. She said she understood now why some Native people were unkind to white people when they wanted to come and participate in ceremonies in South Dakota. She had experienced some discrimination while she was there and she said that she would never take her experiences in the lodge for granted and she would always hold those things sacred because it reminded her of how much work she had to do to regain her centre and her connection with her own ancestors. She regretted not even knowing where her own ancestors were buried. I thought that was a touching conversation to be having at the funeral of the man who had run the lodge that started her on that path.

Archie and Jose—Josephine, Archie's daughter—went to Europe together. He took her with him to run the lodges for the women. She was totally disgusted by the way the European women fawned over her father. She said they did everything except get on the floor and kiss his feet. Jose is about the age of my daughter, so when she was born I was in her mom's Archie's life and she grew up with my girls. Josie was very close to her father. He used to talk about her aunt, the aunt she was named after. When she grew up, he wanted her to know the ceremonies and he taught her and kept her close. When he died, he had a headdress that belonged to his father and some of those feathers belonged to his grandfather, so it had passed down through the family. He used to talk about how he hadn't really been prepared to take the pipe when his father died. His son John was married to a non-Native woman and had a little girl. At the funeral, that headdress and the title of chief was passed onto John. Josephine was really hurt. She said, "I should be the one taking those feathers. I should be the one being acknowledged as chief, but it won't happen because I'm a woman." I looked at her and I could see in her eyes the determination she had to be able to say that— to be able to express that out loud.

I looked at her and said, "You are more than a chief. You are a leader." She laughed and gave me a hug.

It's disturbing how women, no matter what their training, no matter what they have learned as they've grown, are still not acknowledged, and are still not honoured, nor respected. The Womyn's Sundance is a place where I have always envisioned empowering women, empowering women to be able to go back to their communities and run lodges. Someone used the term rainbow lodge, meaning lodges for people of all colours. Some people call these the four-directions lodges because recently Orville Looking Horse posted a letter on the Internet about how only Lakota people should be running lodges, and only if you speak your own tribal language should you be in the lodge, without thinking about the fact that eighty per cent, if not more, of the Native people left on this continent are of mixed blood. You cannot stop two people from falling in love and having a child. When you have these children of mixed blood and you say that only someone who speaks their own language can come into the lodge, well, English might be their own and only language. The important thing is where your prayers come from, that they come from your heart, where you are in the lodge, when you go into that lodge. If we don't hang onto the ceremonies and hold them for our children to learn, we're going to lose them.

I've always been taught that when the door to the lodge is closed, it doesn't matter what colour you are, it doesn't matter what you have, what you don't have, who you are, who you think you are. It's pitch black in that lodge. The only thing that Spirit is looking at is your heart. When that door is closed, we are all one. There is no difference between us in the dark. A lot of people criticize when white people go into the lodge. A lot of people criticize when women are pouring water in the lodge. But it's time for women to step into those roles. It's time for us to be able to teach our daughters and our sons because a lot of the men are not available to do that. They are not always there to do that. They're busy writing big long letters to post on the Internet. I consider Orville Looking Horse one of our leaders. His heart is in a good direction. I hear his concern for the environment, his concern for the Lakota people, but there is also that edge of criticism of other people. I was told long ago during one of my vision fasts—and I have done four vision fasts—that we are not in a position as two-legged to judge anything or anybody.

That has probably been by far the hardest challenge of my lifetime and I still continue to walk on it—not to judge someone's actions or where someone is at. We'll say, oh, I'm not judgmental. Someone walks in the room and they're wearing two different colours that clash, and we think, wow, they sure don't know their colours. That's making a judgment. I am constantly being challenged in that way. I know there are things that come out of my mouth that sound like judgments and I have to watch out for those. I have to look at those so that I'm constantly aware of them. My grandma said that Lakota people never called themselves medicine men or medicine women. They didn't call themselves healers, they didn't call themselves shaman. Those were the words of the white man. That among the Lakota—and it is reflected in the Lakota language—you were labeled that way by others. In our language, if someone comes to you and asks, "What is your name?" it translates to: "What are you called?" Your response to that is, "My people call me.... My people call me Beverly." Oftentimes people will say, "You're a healer, you're a teacher," and I'll say, "No, I'm not. I'm not. That's not what I am." If I'm willing to accept that and accept that people are going to look at me that way, then I also need to look at myself and make myself worthy of that, and becoming worthy means not judging. Becoming worthy means teaching a lot by example and teaching by storytelling, which I think I do. It's taken a long time for me to accept what I do. But nowhere in my life contract—and I've looked, believe me, I've looked at it with a fine comb—do I have instructions that say I get to be a judge. I don't get to judge, even if someone kills another person. I don't get to judge. I can't say, what that person did was wrong, or what that person did was good. They did what they felt they had to do and they will face the consequences of their actions.

When I was with my grandmother, she explained something to me: for every action, there's a reaction; for everything you do, you set the wheels in motion for something else to happen, and there are two sides of everything. So I grew up knowing that if I didn't see the sky as blue as it is right now with the sun shining, I couldn't appreciate that sky if I hadn't seen it on a day when there were lots of clouds and lots of rain and it was cold and windy. So, you can't appreciate the things that are beautiful if you haven't seen the things that are ugly, and if you do something that you think is good for someone, you have to know that there will be someone else who is going to look upon that action as not being good. There's always going to be that opposite. Everything has two sides to it. Sometimes in the lodge I say, be careful what you ask for, you might get it. That's what I'm talking about when I say that, because that's what I have learned.

Many women throughout their lives, in the last hundred years, have not been taught these things. We have had to find these things out for ourselves. We have had to figure them out for ourselves. Part of what I learned as I was growing, from my mother, who was not a spiritual person outwardly, from my grandmother, who was also not a spiritual person outwardly, and from the other women in my life, is that we need to be able to talk to each other. We need to be able to empower each other. In our western civilization this has been lacking and that's why we have had movements like the suffrage movement, women who banded together for the vote, the women's liberation movement of the seventies and onward, and all of the subsequent movements to empower women. Women have been, and still are, hungry for empowerment. In many of these movements, one or two Native women may have been participated, but Native women, on the whole, kind of stepped back, because we were told that that it wasn't our place, as Native women.

The European invasion of this continent changed our entire culture. The way that our men looked at us changed. The white man came and said, "This is my wife, who cooks and cleans for me and that's about it. What do you mean you're bringing your wife to a council fire? We don't want them. This is men's talk. We decide. We're the men. We take care of the women." It had a huge impact on how our Native men looked at us.

Drugs and alcohol have had a tremendous impact on Native families. Five hundred years or more of that kind of infiltration has completely changed Native culture, tradition, and society. Every tribe on this continent has changed. As women, we now need to reach inside our memory and pull the memory of our traditions and the values, the values that our people had, to the forefront. With the Sundance and empowering women, that's what I have worked to do. It's not how you do the dance in the arbor, what steps you take, if you turn right or left. There is a protocol for how you go through the dance and over the years it might change. These are not the important things. The important things are the values that we are reclaiming. One of the core values is honesty and following through with commitment. Another core value is listening to Spirit and knowing, knowing that Spirit can talk through you, knowing that you can hear Spirit, knowing that Spirit exists and surrounds you, all the time. So many people don't realize that. They think they have to read a book about it to learn. They think they have to be given permission to make those connections.

When people come to me and ask for teachings to pour the water, I teach them. I teach them why we build the lodge the way we build it and all the little nuances that go with it, and even as I do that, I know that some of those things will change. A hundred years from now, some of them will change. But what I don't want to change is why they are done. Someone is going to say, why are we using tobacco in our ceremony? I too have questioned why we use tobacco when I see millions of people dying who smoke tobacco. Millions of people's lives have been affected and changed because of the chemicals in tobacco, and yet we continue to offer that tobacco to the ground. Are we offering poison to our Mother Earth? I have seriously considered stopping the use of tobacco and using cornmeal, or using something else that is organic. These are things that someone is going to have the courage to change, some day. Someone's going to say, okay, enough of this. As a woman, I think that's my responsibility. It's the responsibility of all women to question. To question why we do the things what we do, and then to weigh the benefit of that.

PLANTING SEEDS OF HOPE

A number of years ago, I was asked to come to a spring equinox ceremony. I went to the store and as I was shopping, I noticed that they had already put up their seed displays, so I grabbed several packages of seeds. Some were seeds for squash, some were for pumpkin, and some were for cucumbers. I went home and grabbed a bunch of yogurt cups. There were going to be about twenty women at the ceremony, so I punched little holes into the bottoms of twenty cups, filled them with soil, and then pushed all the various seeds down into the dirt. I didn't know which ones were cucumber, which ones were pumpkin, which ones were squashes—I think there were watermelons seeds too— because once they were in the dirt, they all looked alike. I tied little ribbons around them to make the little yogurt cups look fancy. I went to the ceremony and at the end of the ritual, I did a giveaway. I gave away all these little yogurt cups of seeds. I instructed the women to take them home and water them and see what grew, and that the next time we met, I would ask them to tell me about their plants.

The next time we met was almost a year later. Not all the women were there, but there were quite a few of them. So, I asked, what did you grow? How did your little seedlings do? There was only one woman there whose seedling had grown to the point where she could plant it outside in her garden and it had yielded her about ten squash, which she ate throughout the winter. Everyone else said, "Well, I started watering it. It sprouted and it got to be about four inches tall and then I forgot to water it and it died." Someone else said, "I live in the city, so I set it out on the landing, on the fire escape, and it got knocked over by a cat and it died." Or, "I transplanted it out in the yard and then I forgot it was there. I never watered it and it died." Out of all the ones I had given out that night, only one had survived. Without chastising anyone, I said, "This is how we, as women, have been taught to take care of the earth in our time. Let this be a lesson that we need to do better. How are we going to teach our children these things if we can't do them ourselves? How are we going to create plans in our lives for what we teach our children? How do we teach our children?" I was very sad to hear that only one had survived, that only one woman was successful, but I was really glad to hear that at least she got to eat some squash. If we had all been out in the bush and each of us had one seed and we had to depend on that seed to feed us through the winter, we would of had nineteen starving women, nineteen starving families. If they'd all had children, they would have starved.

These are the simple things that I believe as women we need to teach each other, that we need to remind each other of. These are the kind of things I talk about when I talk about values. The value of the earth. The value of what is around us. We may think we are, but we are not the most important thing on the planet. We are not superior, even if that's what we've been taught. We've been taught that we are the superior intelligence. But we need to know that we are not. Most women will say, "Well, I know that I'm not." Most women will say they feel a connection with the earth, but they don't know how to work within that framework. When I started the Womyn's Sundance, I took a risk in performing that ceremony. I asked no one's permission to do it. There were many men, I am certain, who said, well, she has no right to do that. And I probably didn't have the right to do that, if anyone at all has to have "the right" to do anything. But I was taught the steps of that dance and I understood the steps of that dance. And I don't just mean the steps to take as you are walking through the arbor. With those steps, the steps that I was taught, also came the responsibility of passing those steps on. As a woman, I choose to pass the steps on to my sisters. I choose to help the next generations to follow in those steps and to pray for that, because I don't think we have much of a choice. It's going to be women who will transform this planet. The men have made a big mess of it.

CHILDREN ARE GIFTS LOANED TO US BY CREATOR

As women, we are the ones responsible for teaching the children. We are the ones who teach our boys, our sons. We are the first females our sons connect with. Some of our sons get caught up by the patriarchal mindset, but I don't believe they ever lose their core connection to their mothers. I look at my son, my youngest son. He is a big guy. There are some times when he is so macho because he feels that's what he needs to be. He's a man. Then there's other times when he's nothing but a big teddy bear, and he is in awe of simple things, like the sun setting, or watching the horses run, or going out and taking photographs of a pig. He can be taking photos of a chicken, or teaching a little boy that that's where eggs come from. He is a very gentle soul. He is an incredible man. But when he's being his macho self, it's hard to be around him. As women, part of our responsibility on this planet is to teach our boys, our men. Whether we have biological children or not, we are all mothers, to all children, and grandmothers, to all children, and, as such, we have a responsibility.

As I said earlier, when Lakota children were born, mothers kept their children close, because they usually breastfed them until they were about four or five. After that, if they were male, they were sent to live with their uncles and their grandfather, who continued their teaching, and Mom was just there to love them. Cook for them. Maybe make clothes for them. But she had nothing to do with their discipline, nothing to do with their teaching. The men were going to take care of that. If they were little girls, they usually stayed close to their moms, but they were also swept up by grandmas and aunties and other females and they were taught other skills—how to make moccasins, how to skin a hide, how to pack up a teepee when you are getting ready to move, how to gather berries, how to save berries, how to recognize different herbs, how to recognize which plants are edible and those that are not. It was a joint effort. It truly took a village to raise a child. And again, all the mother had to do was love that child, so there was never any animosity toward the mother because she was only seen as the nurturer, not the disciplinarian. That's not how it is in our society right now. Many mothers now have to be both the nurturer and the disciplinarian. It is much harder. It's no wonder that we have kids who turn eighteen and rebel; kids who take off and think they want to be on their own because they feel smothered by someone whose whole role has been to love them, to nurture them, and to teach them.

I do not believe this society values children. This society has stuck women into little pigeon holes and said, "Okay, you have children. These are *your* children. *You're* responsible for them." And we, as women, as mothers, have bought that. We believe that. We refer to children as *my* children. In the Lakota language, there's no word for "mine." We don't take ownership of things. It's not "mine." This is the pipe. This isn't *my* pipe, it's *the* pipe. These eagle feathers. They're not *my* eagle feathers. I'm honoured to carry these feathers. I don't own them, but I have been honoured to carry them, I have been honoured with them. I think if we really had the time—and there are some people out there who do—to study languages, we would see a real big difference between the Lakota language and the English language, where everything is "mine." This belongs to me. This is mine. These are *my* children. This is *my* house. This is *my* garden. This is *my* food. This is *my* horse. All those things belong to us—that's a lot of responsibility for us to take, I think. No wonder people have mental breakdowns. No wonder women feel overwhelmed. A poor young woman recently strangled her two children. Then she strapped them into their car seats and pushed her car into a lake. She tried to claim that her children had drowned because she realized that she'd be in trouble. Now she has to live with that guilt. She has to live with the knowledge that she took the lives of these two innocent children who'd been gifted to her.

Children are gifts to us, and whether we bear them or not, they're in our lives. They're watching everything we do and you never know when something that you do is going to affect a child as that child grows up. It might be something they watched you do, or it might be something they heard. Even if we don't talk to these children, they're still watching us, they're still listening. So, as women, we need to recognize our power. We need to be aware of the power that we hold and we need to be able to hold that power in a way that doesn't emulate the patriarchal system. Men recognize they have power. They recognize in many situations they have power and that becomes something they can use, something that will increase their power. As women, we don't need more power. We have all the power that we need. And we need to use that power to give to our communities, to give to the earth.

LIFE IS A PRAYER, A CEREMONY

One time I had a woman from California come and stay with me. She'd been with me about a week when she said, "I was really scared to come here, Beverly." I asked her why. She said, "I was told that you Lakota are really strict and that every day you get up and do ceremony. I'm not a morning person. I don't get up until nine, ten o'clock."

I said, "I don't get up until about seven, eight o'clock."

She said, "Yeah, but I always miss ceremony."

I said, "I do ceremony every morning. You've sat at the table while I've done ceremony."

She said, "I have?"

I have a small altar sitting in our living area. I have an altar in my bedroom, but I also have an altar in our living area. I said to the visiting woman, "Every morning I get up and I walk over to the altar and light a candle if there's not a candle already lit. I burn sage and I offer a prayer. I go over to the sink, get a glass of water and I offer water. I drink some water and then I say a prayer. I don't have plants on my windowsill in my kitchen that are planted in dirt. They're all being rooted and I offer my water there each morning. Eventually I take those plants and I put them in soil. Then I replace them with new cuttings. Do I go outside? Do I stand there with my hands in the air and pray and turn around and drum? No. I've been known to do that for special occasions, but not on a day-to-day basis." She just looked at me. She thought that was really odd, based on what she'd heard. But what she'd heard was a stereotype. I told her, "I don't know anybody who does that—goes and stands outside and drums and sings and does a whole ritual like that every morning. In the world we live in today, most of us live in a city. We'd get run down by a streetcar if we went out in the middle of the road and tried to do that. But, there is always the value, the understanding that my life is ceremony, and that each thing that I do has an effect on something. I make a difference in everything that I do, every day. We all do."

I like to tell the story about the starfish, about the little girl who picked up the starfish and threw if back into the ocean, and said, "I made a difference in that one's life." Every one of us makes a difference. Every one of us picks up the starfish and throws it back in the ocean in some way, some form. We make a difference in the lives of everybody we meet. It might be a stranger walking down the street who we greet with a smile. That might be the only smile that person gets all day. That might make the difference between that person continuing with their lives or putting a bullet in their head. We don't know. We will never know. Western society teaches us that we have to see the outcome of our actions to know if those actions have been successful. We are told we have to measure success and success is measured by what we can see or what we can touch. Native people, however, do not measure our values and our success in these ways. These things are measured by the knowledge that we've done the right thing, that we've done the best we can.

Those values come back to personal responsibility. Western society has given fancy names to so many things that we, as Native people have implemented in our lifestyles for centuries, without having given them fancy names. Native people today have been given the additional burden of having to maintain those values through the web of—excuse the word—crap, that's been dumped on us. The physical and sexual abuse of children was never heard of before the European people came to this continent. Our children were valued. Our children were important. Children are the ones who will carry the future. They are the ones who will feed us when we got old. Family is really important, and not just mom and dad and son and daughter. Family includes aunties, uncles, cousins. In Lakota tradition, beyond an aunt and uncle, everybody's a grandma. Everybody's a grandpa. A child could have umpteen million aunties and umpteen million grandmas. Even in my family, my mother's sisters are my grannies, my grandmothers. They're not my aunties; they are my grandmothers. Family is anybody who's in your circle and you treat them and honour them and respect them as family. It's a different way of thinking about family than the way white people think about family. White people like to box everything in.

Through colonization, Native people have been subject to that train of thought, too, so we've also learned to start to box things in. I think we are at a time now when women all over the world are realizing how detrimental that is, not only to life, but to the planet, for she is responsible for all we have. Will Native people, Native values, save the earth? I don't know. Perhaps Mother Earth is meant to self-destruct. I have kicked and screamed and thrown myself on the ground and asked Creator to give me a glimpse of what's to come, to show me how what I do now is going to impact a hundred years in the future. And all Creator has done is laugh. Creator hasn't given me that insight and hasn't shown me what is to come. I am not supposed to know. I am on a need-to-know basis. But as women, we need to be ready when we are told what we need to do. The ego that embraces the male counterpart really has no room in a matriarchal society. We cannot afford to think of ourselves as superior to someone else. We cannot afford to think of ourselves as knowing more than someone else. We may have been taught otherwise, and we may even have a little more knowledge, but that knowledge isn't ours to keep. It's ours to pass on. In Lakota tradition the men pass knowledge from man to man. They don't pass knowledge to women. But today this is often different. Today, many men pass on knowledge to women and women also pass on knowledge to the men.

MY HEALING THROUGH CEREMONY

My healing process is tied to my spirituality. I'm not even sure where one ends and where the other begins. It just is. During my first vision fast, I was terrified because I'm afraid of being alone and in the dark. I feared a wild boar would get me. I feared a man who was hiking would stumble upon me. I was really scared. I had to face my fears. When I came off the hill, I felt much better. Fear certainly gives you something to pray for. Fear also provides a way to take a deep inner look into yourself, to force you to look at what your behaviours are, which ones you need and which ones you don't, which ones to let go of. During that vision fast, I could see all the protections and walls I had put up around myself. I had to tear a lot of those walls down. I now believe that I am valuable. I believe I am important to this planet and everything I do impacts somebody. It may not affect the masses, but it affects one person. It affects that starfish. I make a difference in this one's life. And that's got to be enough, because I'm never going to get to all the millions and millions of starfish. I don't even care if people know what my name is, as long as they remember something I said that helped them. My spirituality has been very important to that healing process.

I used to go to Sunday school and they would have something they called "altar calls." You'd be called to the altar and they'd say, Jesus is going to touch you, and you will feel all these wonderful things. Jesus is going to touch you and you'll be filled with the Holy Ghost. It didn't matter how much I prayed. It didn't matter how sincere I was. I never felt anything touch me. I was never filled with anything, except dread. But from my first time in the lodge, I felt Spirit. I felt Spirit fill me and take care of me. It's a hard thing. People will ask me what they will experience in the sweat lodge. I think it's different for everybody. But that's how it was for me. That's how I knew that's where I needed to be. If I have my way, that's where I'll die. Dying in a lodge would be the best! Of course, my family has different ideas, but families always see things differently. Your children especially. They don't want mom to ever die.

Spirituality is when you start delving deeper and deeper into the values you have in this world—that's all that I see spirituality as—a connection to the Creator. Spirituality is something much bigger than all of us. And it dictates what I do in my life. It's definitely a service job. I've had a lot of different health issues come up in my life. I've had cancer three times. I've been in therapy three times. I've always had high blood pressure. I have diabetes. Most recently, I've had back issues—three discs have collapsed in my spine and they have had to be fused together. Each time, I have felt it was a message from Spirit telling me something more that I needed to do, something that I wasn't doing that I should have been doing. I don't view any of these things as terrible catastrophes that have been following me. I tend to look at these things, like, okay, how do I revamp my life and continue doing the work I need to do in a different way? I think sometimes the pain that we hold inside and the dysfunction that has permeated our lives can manifest as cancers or some of these other illnesses. So, I really look at these things and ask, okay, what's going on?

Whenever I'm in a situation where I've had a lot of responsibility, my shoulders start hurting and my neck starts hurting and for me this is symbolic of trying to carry the load on your shoulders all by yourself. Once I recognize that and start making some changes—for example, disburse and spread some of the responsibility—the pain goes away. I think your body tells you a lot about what's going on. Sometimes chronic illnesses, for me, are reminders that reign me in to where I need to be, and to what I need to be doing. I believe everything is interconnected and I believe that when Creator takes one ability away, we're given another. Then I find another way of doing the same work, but doing it on a different level.

Ceremony has been by far the most important aspect of my life because it's taught me so many different values. The most important thing I have learned is that I don't have the right to judge anyone, even the people who violated me. I don't have to like what they did, but I don't have to label them as bad people. I recognize that they were probably injured and hurt in their lifetimes and that's why they felt the need to inflict that kind of pain on someone else. Like I said, it always gives me something to pray for. There's never a lack of things to pray for. And the healing that has taken place has led me to today and to my relationship with Pam. I really never thought I'd be in a relationship with a white woman, never mind with a healthy woman.

My prayer had always been to bring a Native woman into my life—one that understands all the different bullet points. I never thought about bringing a healthy white woman into my life. So when Charlene came, she came with all her baggage and all her baggage resulted in me becoming her punching bag. In looking back on it and having done a lot of praying and healing, I realized that she too was molested as a child. She talked about her molestation to me a couple of times and I could see where her anger would stem from and how it could be misguided and inappropriately vented on someone else. In that understanding, I was able to develop compassion and forgive her—not forget, but to forgive her.

Ceremony has taught me a lot about forgiveness, about learning to forgive myself, and what that really means. It means more than just saying, I'm sorry. It means coming to peace within oneself and I have finally have achieved that. It's a good place to be. It's a really good place to be.

My life has been a journey of one step at a time. Each painful experience was tempered by something that brought hope and joy. For each person who has not been there for me, there has been another who has been. At age five, I watched both my mother and my aunt doing bead work. I begged them to teach me. First I had to learn to thread the needle, and then I learned how to string the beads. Finally, my aunt created a small loom out of a shoe box with combs taped to the ends. With practice I learned to combine colours and create patterns in my work. My mother told me in later years that she was happy I had learned also the lessons that came with the skill of bead work. Surprised I asked, "What were those lessons?" And she replied that they were patience, perseverance, and pride in my accomplishments. Those skills have helped me move through my life in the face of all adversity. They have helped me to be at peace with helping empower one woman at a time, and to insist that failure is not an option.

Placing one bead at a time, planting one seed at a time, and taking one step at a time—like the young girl with the star fish—I know I can make a difference in each life I touch: one person at a time.

Acknowledgements

A huge *pilamiya* (thank you) to Sharron Proulx-Turner for her determination that this book should be written, my daughter Lushanya, for her love and support, and my partner Pam Alexander, who knows all my strengths and weaknesses, yet loves and supports me anyway. This is written for all of the women in my life who have made it so rich and fulfilling. And, finally, thank you to the children, and those who are not yet born, who inspire me and give me hope for a peaceful world one day.

Beverly Little Thunder, Lakota Elder and women's activist, is a member of the Standing Rock Lakota Band from North Dakota. When she was forced to leave her Spiritual community because she was a lesbian, Beverly founded the Women's Sundance over twenty years ago to continue teaching the traditions and ceremonies of her heritage. She currently works with women and children from her Vermont home by teaching leadership skills through the Lakota Sundance ceremony, the sweat lodge ceremony, awareness of and respect for the animal and natural worlds, community talking circles, communication workshops, personal retreats, vision quests, and spiritual counselling.

Sharron Proulx-Turner lives in Calgary and is a member of the Métis Nation of Alberta. She is a two-spirit *nokomis*, mom, writer and community worker. Her previously published memoir, *Where the Rivers Join: A Personal Account of Healing from Ritual Abuse* (1995), written under the pseudonym Beckylane, was a finalist for the Edna Staebler award, and her second book, *what the auntys say* (2002), was a finalist for the League of Canadian Poets' Gerald Lampert Prize. Her 2008 poetry book, *she is reading her blanket with her hands* (2008), was shortlisted for the Governor General Award. She is also the author of *She Walks for Days/ Inside a Thousand Eyes/ A Two-Spirit Story* (2008) and *the trees are still bending south* (2012).